If you have children at home, discussing marriage without examining the way kids impact your relationship is like trying to explain skiing without mentioning snow. Patrick and P...................often-overlooked aspect of marri..................._Better or for Kids._ I wish Lisa and.................look at how a married couple ca.................older when our kids were young.

Gary Thomas, Author of _Sacred Marriage_ and _Sacred Parenting_

In a countercultural move, _For Better or for Kids_ addresses an increasing epidemic in modern American homes—child-centered marriages. With both humor and vulnerability, Ruth and Patrick share how having children changed their marriage—and how learning to focus on each other first not only made them better spouses but also better parents.

Erin Odom, creator of TheHumbledHomemaker.com and
upcoming author with HarperCollins Christian Publishing

For Better or for Kids hooked me as soon as I saw the title. After all, who hasn't struggled with the balance of all it takes to build a strong marriage—at the same time you're trying to raise good kids? But here Patrick and Ruth Schwenk offer us so much wisdom and practical advice for how we can love our spouse well and, yes, even with kids in the house.

Lisa Jacobson, Club31Women.com

For Better or for Kids addresses a huge problem for many modern parents. We have put our kids before our marriages and it's costing us dearly. Parenting requires teamwork, but a husband and wife aren't just co-laborers; they're lovers. Patrick and Ruth will help you keep the promises you made to your beloved _before_ children came along.

Arlene Pellicane, author of _31 Days to a Happy_
Husband and _Growing Up Social_

For Better or for Kids gracefully tackles most of the common challenges married couples face once children enter onto the scene. With transparency, humor, and practical wisdom, Pat and Ruth share a vital message throughout this book: marriages can still thrive with children in the house. This book is a must-read for any married couple with kids!

Mike & Carlie Kercheval, cofounders of FulfillingYourVows.com, coauthors of *Learning to Speak Life™ Family Bible Study Guide*.

After working with couples for over ten years now, I realize the vital need for good resources when a husband and wife welcome kids into their family. *For Better or for Kids* is the book I have been waiting for to recommend to couples as they transition from kidless married adults to mom and dad. In this book, the Schwenks provide biblical truth as they encourage parents to push through in the middle of the challenges (and blessings) of life with children.

Scott Kedersha, Director of Premarital and Newly Married Ministries, Watermark Community Church, scottkedersha.com

Every marriage needs this important parenting book! Children can change things between a husband and wife—for better or worse! This book is a practical and spiritual guide for your marriage as you travel the parenting road. I highly recommend it!

Kristen Welch, author of *Raising Grateful Kids in an Entitled World*

The pastoral wisdom of Pat and the visionary mothering heart of Ruth come together in these much-needed pages for all of us who find ourselves seeking to build our marriages while growing our families. The Schwenks lovingly show us, from within the trenches themselves, that one doesn't have to happen to the detriment of the other. The practical wisdom in this book will meet marriages in the throes of parenting and encourage them to keep their eyes on the prize and press on.

Ruth Chou Simons, mom of six boys, artist, writer, founder of gracelaced.com

If you're married with children, yet struggling to be a united team, I highly recommend *For Better or for Kids*. Patrick and Ruth do a fantastic job of offering biblical encouragement and practical tools that will help strengthen your "team us"!

Ashleigh Slater, author of *Team Us: Marriage Together*

In a day when parenting can become just another task-list entry for young couples, Patrick and Ruth Schwenk offer a needed reality check in *For Better or for Kids*. Theirs is life-learned advice for making the life-changing transition from living like "married singles" to actually being "married with children." With a been-there, learned-that, humorous and conversational style, they remind couples like them who are wondering, "What just happened?" that this is real life — marriage is unavoidably changed by good parenting, parenting is necessarily dependent on a good marriage, and it is all good by God's design.

Clay & Sally Clarkson, authors and speakers on
Christian home and parenting, Whole Heart Ministries,
Mom Heart Ministry, SallyClarkson.com

Marriage vows can feel lyrical and distant when held up against the grit of real life. But in their practical and yet vision-inspiring book, *For Better or for Kids*, Patrick and Ruth Schwenk bridge the gap between what we once said that can feel "way back when" and what we're living now. It's a hope-giving book that offers strength within the pages.

Sara Hagerty, author of *Every Bitter Thing Is Sweet*

It's refreshing to see a real couple dealing with real issues and provide real, "hands-on" advice! Their personal stories provide hope and direction for any weary parent! Patrick and Ruth Schwenk have done a great job encouraging the hearts and minds of parents everywhere, at any phase of life in "for better or for kids."

Clare Smith, writer/speaker/blogger at claresmith.me

For Better or for Kids will inspire—and prod—you to be a real team with your spouse! With humility and humor, Ruth and Patrick share the mistakes they made and the lessons they've learned while "loving your spouse with four kids in the house!" In their stories of busyness, unexpected tragedy, and the mundane of everyday parenting, they always come back to one thing: now that you're parents, your marriage matters more, not less, because other people are counting on you. So cling to each other and get ready for the most exciting ride of your life!

Sheila Wray Gregoire, blogger at ToLoveHonorandVacuum.com and award-winning author of *The Good Girl's Guide to Great Sex*

For Better or for Kids is a must-read for parents everywhere. Through highly relatable and compelling discussion, Ruth and Patrick Schwenk have created a valuable resource that is sure to encourage and equip the heart of every reader.

Becky Thompson, author of *Hope Unfolding and Love Unending*, creator of Scissortail SILK

For Better or for Kids is an honest and pure resource that addresses that familiar and complicated space in marriage between expectation and reality. Patrick and Ruth provide real-life examples and practical steps that not only help close the gap but ultimately align our perspectives with God's purpose and his truth.

Wynter Pitts, founder & author, *For Girls Like You* magazine and devotionals

For Better or for Kids is a must-read for any husband and wife with kids! This is a beautiful resource that encourages the heart of those who are in the throes of parenting. No matter how long you have been married, no matter how old your kids are, this book is for you.

Jennifer Smith, author of *The Unveiled Wife* and founder of Unveiledwife.com

May-31-2016

41452_HNC_1602

Patrick and Ruth Schwenk have an important message to all of us who think we can put our marriage on the back burner once kids come into the family picture. They remind us a good marriage is the key to a healthy family. They know it is not easy but also know it is God's design to put your marriage first. I recommend this book to all the parents who forget what a date night is, fantasize about the days before kids, and who just need to rekindle the fire and commitment to a vibrant marriage in a frenetic season of life. Read this book with your spouse and enjoy this season for all its worth.

Dr. Garrett Higbee, Executive Director of Biblical Soul Care Ministries at Harvest Bible Chapel in Chicago

For better
– OR –
for Kids

A Vow to Love Your Spouse
with Kids in the House

PATRICK AND RUTH SCHWENK

ZONDERVAN

For Better or for Kids
Copyright © 2016 by Patrick and Ruth Schwenk

Requests for information should be addressed to:
Zondervan, 3900 *Sparks Dr. SE, Grand Rapids, Michigan 49546*

ISBN 978-0-310-34274-8 (ebook)

Library of Congress Cataloging-in-Publication Data

Names: Schwenk, Patrick, author.
Title: For better or for kids : a vow to love your spouse with kids in the house /
    Patrick and Ruth Schwenk.
Description: Grand Rapids : Zondervan, 2016.
Identifiers: LCCN 2016007471 | ISBN 9780310342663 (softcover)
Subjects: LCSH: Parents--Religious life. | Marriage--Religious aspects--Christianity.
    | Families--Religious aspects--Christianity. | Families--Religious life.
Classification: LCC BV4529 .S3924 2016 | DDC 248.8/44--dc23 LC record available
    at http://lccn.loc.gov/2016007471

Cover Design: *Studio Gearbox*
Interior design: *Kait Lamphere*

First Printing May 2016/Printed in the United States of America

To our kids in the house:
Tyler, Bella, Noah, and Sophia

You have brought us more joy than you will ever know.
You are arrows in God's hands.
Dream big because your God is big. We love you.

CONTENTS

1

MARRIAGE

It's Not What We Expect,
But It Is Good

True love doesn't happen by accident. It's deliberate,
it's intentional, it's purposeful and in the end . . .
it's worth it.

Darlene Schacht, *Messy Beautiful Love*

The first sign Ruth and I had that our ideal picture of marriage would crumble happened the morning of our wedding. During the early hours of August 8, 1998, I stopped by Ruth's parents' house to pick up a few items. Ruth and her bridesmaids were scurrying from the house to a car waiting to take them to the church. It was barely light outside. The bridal party was a blur amongst the hustle and bustle. However, one image stood out with great clarity—the image of Ruth ducking into the car carrying a large steel cooking pot, the kind of pot you make loads of chili in!

The problem was, Ruth wasn't planning on cooking. She was planning on marrying me. But she was sick! Nauseous, on the verge of throwing up sick!

No! This is our wedding day! I thought. *She can't be sick! This can't be happening!* Although I wanted to let out a cry of anguish, I had enough wisdom to keep my despair to myself.

I had dreamed about this day since I was a sixth-grade boy. Now I admit, my ideal picture had far more to do with raging hormones than ceremony details, perfect weather, incoming family, or the reception menu. In my mind this was the day all the "do nots" finally became the "oh, yes you cans!" This was a big day and a big night. Ruth absolutely could *not* be sick!

Apparently our wedding and, as I would soon discover, our marriage would be different from what I expected.

Okay, heading to the church with a large pot in my lap wasn't quite what I (*Ruth*) had in mind either. I had pictured a beautiful morning with birds singing and laughter in the air— just like the wedding magazines portrayed. I imagined myself casually sauntering about getting ready for the best day of my life. Unfortunately, I had scheduled the wedding to take place at 10:00 a.m.

I am not sure what I was thinking, especially since I am a night owl, not a morning person! Why didn't anyone warn me that getting ready for my wedding would take six hours? I arose at 4:00 a.m. after a restless night's sleep. It was way too early.

Running on about three hours of sleep was not a good way to start the day. As I was getting my hair done, feeling jittery from nervous anticipation of the big day ahead of me, I realized I wasn't feeling well. I was on the verge of losing my cookies—thus the large cooking pot.

In spite of the nerve-racking start, our wedding turned out just fine, but it sure had us both in a panic! That day we experienced the first of what would become many marital reality checks. Each of us enters marriage with a picture of what we hope and expect our marriage to be. As Patrick and I discovered, it usually doesn't take long for that vision of perfection to crumble.

What Were We Expecting?

Relationships begin in many different ways. Ours began with a prank phone call. Yes, that's right! While attending the Moody Bible Institute in Chicago, I (*Patrick*) called Ruth pretending to be a local radio station DJ offering an opportunity to win cash.

The goal was simple: call an unsuspecting student and pretend to be giving away money to the individual who could "dash for the cash" at a particular intersection in downtown Chicago. What poor college student wouldn't jump at such a generous offer? From our tenth-floor dorm window, the view was perfectly entertaining. This, along with other radio contest scenarios, provided much-needed stress relief from our studies.

Ruth didn't fall for the prank, but she did fall for me. I'll be forever grateful to my roommate who suggested we call this unsuspecting classmate of his. That failed prank phone call led to a double date, then another, until finally I had the courage to ask her to be my valentine.

For the longest time we thought marriage would be all about romantic love. After all, that's how it started out. The long walks, meaningful talks, bubbling emotion, eye-gazing, hand-holding type of love. You know, the good stuff we all read about, watch, listen to, and dream about. We had the idea that all married couples naturally have time for romance every night, hold hands during dinner, and hide unexpected love notes to be discovered by the other.

Of course, we knew there was more to marriage than loving affection. As Christians, we knew that marriage had a purpose bigger than just the two of us and that we needed a spiritual foundation for our life together. We knew we had different perspectives and ways of doing things. We knew there was more to marriage than romance, but we weren't too sure what it looked like or how it would impact our life together.

At the time, neither one of us realized how different we were or how those differences would affect our vision and expectation of marriage. Ruth was an only child, a new Christian who grew up in a loving, hardworking, but not Christian family. Pat was a PK (pastor's kid), a lifelong Christian who was raised with two older sisters in a conservative Christian home and church in the Midwest. One of us was an extrovert, the other an introvert. One was a spender, the other a saver. One was an optimist, the other a pessimist. In short, we faced plenty of obstacles trying to navigate the choppy waters of relational harmony.

For our premarital counseling, we called Ruth's pastor, who would be doing our wedding. He was the father of one of Ruth's closest friends in high school. After our first session, he sent us home with instructions to complete Norman Wright's classic workbook, *Before You Say "I Do."* If you aren't familiar with this book, it is full of helpful and biblical wisdom to get couples started on the right path. We know this because that is what the back cover promised.

We made it through lesson one.

The plan was to work through the workbook one lesson a week. Week one was anything but enjoyable! I (*Patrick*) remember thinking, *I thought this was going to be fun.* Eager to get a good start and hopeful that week two would be better, we cracked open the book again. We sat on the floor of Ruth's family room, looked over a few notes from the previous week, and began the study. We had good intentions, but lesson two stopped us in our tracks. Ironically, in a discussion about acceptance in marriage, I erupted in anger and marched out of the room! We never did finish the book.

We were oblivious to them at the time, but our differences were already causing significant division between us. We were a bit naive and surprised that the sacred bond of marriage God created didn't just happen. We never suspected that something so good would take so much work to fully enjoy. It was going to take far more than finishing a workbook to live out God's purpose for our relationship. In time, however, we would learn that being intentional about living out God's vision for our marriage would be worth it.

Snapshot of Our Early Years

Considering the progress we made in premarital counseling, it may not surprise you that our first few years of marriage were filled with a lot of trial and a whole lot of error. They were a mixture of excitement, hormones, fear, frustration, adventure, and a lot of immaturity. We still have a picture that I (*Ruth*) took of Patrick in the middle of an argument on our honeymoon. It summarizes our experience well. It was one of those arguments, like most, that when you look back seems silly at best. We were heading out to eat and the conversation went something like this:

Patrick: "Where do you want to eat at tonight, honey?"
Ruth: "It doesn't matter."
Patrick: "Well, what sounds good?"
Ruth: "I'm not sure."
Patrick: "How about restaurant _____?"
Ruth: "No, that doesn't sound good, but if you want to go there we can."
Patrick: (*Avoiding the obvious pitfall*) "No, that's okay. How about restaurant _____?"
Ruth: (*Feeling reluctant*) "No, that doesn't really sound good either."
Patrick: (*Becoming increasingly less like Jesus and lacking in relational wisdom*) "Apparently you do care where we eat! Since you care so much, why don't you choose?"

As Patrick forcefully stepped on the accelerator, the look on his face, his voice, his body language, and increasing speed said it all: He was mad! Honestly, I found it a bit humorous—so humorous that I pulled out my camera to capture the moment. Out of the corner of his eye Patrick realized he was being photographed, but by the time he figured it out, it was too late. The moment and memory are forever captured on film. The picture is still in our scrapbook as a reminder of how silly and selfish some of our interactions were during those early years.

Like a glass of ice-cold water being dumped on you during a hot shower, the reality of married life shocked us. Yes, it was painful. The crumbling of what we thought a perfect marriage would be captured our full attention. We knew something wasn't right, and we longed for something more, something better. If we were going to have a God-honoring marriage, we knew it was going to have to be a God-informed marriage. Our desire for love and relationship had to be built on God's Word if it was going to work. So we made a deliberate choice to start, or restart, our relationship according to God's purpose.

Piecing Together a Better Picture

I (*Ruth*) grew up putting puzzles together. It was one of my grandfather's favorite hobbies. It was not uncommon to walk into my grandparents' house and find thousands of pieces spread out on a table. Some of my fondest memories with my grandparents were the hours spent carefully searching for a puzzle piece to put in its appropriate spot. It was not an easy job, but I loved it when the puzzle was completed!

What draws me into a puzzle is the picture on the box cover. It gives me that first glimpse of what I will build and inspires me to go for it. Without the guiding image on the box cover, it would be nearly impossible to know what the finished picture is supposed to be, let alone how all the pieces are supposed to fit together. The picture on the cover gets me excited and gives me direction as I get to work.

Often in marriage (and in marriage books) we pay a lot of attention to the individual "pieces." We focus on improving communication, intimacy, conflict resolution, roles, finances—the list goes on. These, of course, are all important and necessary pieces of the marriage puzzle, and we'll cover some of them in this book. But first we need to look at the "box cover." Just like a puzzle, we need to start by seeing the overall picture of marriage as God designed it so we can know and be excited about what we are trying to build.

If we want the kind of marriage God wants for us, we have to align our understanding of marriage with the picture given to us in the Bible. This is what John Stott means when he says:

> The marriage bond is more than a human contract: it is a divine yoke. And the way in which God lays this yoke upon a married couple is not by creating a kind of mystical union but by declaring his purpose in his Word.[1]

The picture of marriage in God's Word declares this sacred bond to be good, very good. It is a picture with purpose. We weren't created to just get by. The gift of marriage was meant to be a blessing. The longing for love, belonging, unity, intimacy, and purpose are meant for us to enjoy together as we align our marriage with God's Word. So let's see what is good about the sacred bond God has created for our benefit and his purpose.

Rediscovering the Goodness of God's Purpose for Marriage

In Genesis 1, God looks at Adam and essentially says, "You're good, but you're not quite done yet." God saw that something was missing in Adam. He was alone and needed a life companion or friend. So God did Adam a tremendous favor when he blessed him with Eve to be his loving, wise, powerful, and intimate partner in life. She would know him, love him, complete him, and share life for God's purposes with him. He

---

1. John Stott, *Issues Facing Christians Today* (Grand Rapids: Zondervan, 2006), 370.

would be her lover, protector, provider, and leader. Together, they would be God's people living for God's purposes.

It was God's design to join a man and a woman together in marriage for lifelong love, relationship, companionship, and friendship, and God declared marriage to be good, very good:

> So the LORD God caused the man to fall into a deep sleep; and while he was sleeping, he took one of the man's ribs and then closed up the place with flesh. Then the LORD God made a woman from the rib he had taken out of the man, and he brought her to the man. The man said, "This is now bone of my bones and flesh of my flesh; she shall be called 'woman,' for she was taken out of man." That is why a man leaves his father and mother and is united to his wife, and they become one flesh. Adam and his wife were both naked, and they felt no shame. (Genesis 2:21–25)

What a beautiful picture! The first "giving of the bride" was not in a church, but in the garden of Eden. God looked at Adam and realized he was ill prepared to do life alone. So he graced him with a woman who would be his wife and friend. It is not by accident that God gifts us with one another. God gives Eve to a man he knows will desperately need her to do life. And she will need him. Together they complement each other. Together they are well suited to face the joys and sorrows of the life ahead of them.

I (*Patrick*) love the response from Adam. I am relieved to discover that there is something biblical about sappy love songs and poems. Adam sees Eve and is so overcome by the Father's gift that he breaks into a poem: "This is now bone of my bones and flesh of my flesh; she shall be called 'woman,' for she was taken out of man."

God, not only in grace but also in wisdom, has "gifted" us with our spouse. When we are challenged by the stresses of life, our spouse might not always seem like God's good, wise, and gracious gift to us. But to keep in focus the vision of our marriage as a gift of friendship and companionship from God, we need to value and treat our spouse as our most important relationship.

I sometimes wonder how different my marriage would be if I consistently saw Ruth as God's gift to me. How might our relationship be different if I saw her as a friend instead of a foe when we have to reconcile our differences? How might our marriage be better if I saw her as one who complements me instead of competes with me when we face difficult challenges? I want to experience how different my marriage can be when I see Ruth as a beautiful daughter of God who reflects more and more of his image and glory.

I (*Ruth*) want to see what my marriage can look like when I truly see Patrick as a gift from God to me. I want to gently prize him in the way I interact with him. Just envisioning what God has designed for us makes me want to put every piece of the marriage puzzle in its appointed place.

Marriage, unlike anything else, joins two individuals as one. Genesis 2:24 says that after the man and woman were joined to each other in marriage, they enjoyed a deep, intimate relationship: "That is why a man leaves his father and mother and is united to his wife, and they become one flesh."

"One flesh," the writer says. A husband and a wife, while distinct, become intimately joined. They become "one flesh." This culmination of oneness is a total giving of ourselves to

Just the *Two* of Us

Take a few moments to talk about the ways you and your spouse are a gift to each other.

- In what ways did God bless you with a great gift when he gave you your spouse?
- What is it about who your spouse is and the things your spouse does that supplies strength in your areas of weakness?

each other in the sacred bond of marriage. One flesh is not just physical or sexual. We will certainly share our bodies, but we also share our possessions, dreams, struggles, insights, abilities, sufferings, and successes. In marriage, God joins us together as an inseparable team—spiritually, relationally, physically, and emotionally. United, we share in living out God's purpose and intent for marriage and family.

It is not surprising then to see that when sin entered the garden, Adam and Eve turned on each other. When they broke God's rule, they also broke relationship. Their sin separated them from God and from each other. From that point on, their relationship would be different. Intimacy and friendship would not come naturally. Both would be possible, but intimacy and friendship would have to be worked for, cultivated, and protected.

While we all experience a crumbling of expectations in marriage, we can view that as a reality check with hope. Oneness is not achieved easily, but there is always a way back to the good plan God desires and intends for us. The pieces really can be put together to build a relationship of beauty, power, friendship, oneness, and purpose. As a couple, we must view our marriage as this kind of inseparable team—a picture of living for God and for each other.

Marriage will not always be what we expected or dreamed of, but marriage by God's design and for God's purposes is good—very good! This sacred bond with intimate companionship and divine purpose is worth every ounce of energy required to hope for and work toward.

2

MARRIAGE WITH CHILDREN

A Mess with a Mission

Precious, no doubt, are these little ones in your eyes; but if you truly love them, then often think about their souls.

J. C. Ryle, *The Duties of Parents*

I have to run to the store," Ruth said.

It was a fall Saturday afternoon, which doesn't mean much unless you are a zealous football fan. Saturdays are for football—Michigan football! "No worries," I said. "Just don't be gone too long. Kickoff is at three thirty, and I still need to mow the yard."

We only had two kids at the time. Tyler was just turning four and Bella had just turned two. They were both too young to be left unattended for any length of time. How long? I wasn't sure, but I was about to find out. Tyler, as most firstborns are, was our rule follower. Bella? Not so much! She didn't always see things quite as black and white as her older brother did!

As the minutes passed and game time grew closer, I was growing antsy about getting the lawn mowed before the game. We had plans after the game, and my window of opportunity was quickly closing.

So I decided to go for it. "Dad needs you guys to stay in the house while he mows the lawn," I instructed. "Tyler, you stay in your room. Bella, you stay in your room." Showing some responsibility, I got out some Legos for Tyler and left Bella playing "dress up" with her dolls.

Rushing outside, I fired up the mower and began moving at lightning speed. Realizing the clock was ticking, I not only needed to get done before kickoff, I needed to get done before Ruth returned. As I mowed the last stretch in the front yard, I spotted Ruth's car. I had been mowing for only ten minutes. She was just coming over the railroad tracks a block from our house. She turned right toward our driveway, and as I turned left to wave, out of the corner of my eye I spotted Bella, obviously no longer in the house! Holding a bright yellow umbrella and singing at the top of her lungs, she walked down the sidewalk toward me. There was just one problem. She was naked. Apparently during "dress up" she decided to "dress down" and go for a walk in the "rain." Ruth didn't have to say a word. I could tell by the look in her eyes—I was in trouble!

Children are a lot of fun, a bit unpredictable, and of course, a blessing. They also throw a whole new wrench into marriage. As much as children enrich a marriage, they can also drastically change it! They bring a whole new dynamic to the picture. You and your spouse now live with the reality of a different person (or persons) in the middle of your marriage. At some point, a loving, hopeful, and energetic married couple find themselves in a minivan loaded with kids and littered with Cheerios, crusty sippy cups, and dark banana peels. Amidst a baffling array of new sounds, different smells, unpredictable schedules, competing preferences, and unusual demands, you can't help but think, *What just happened? We are in way over our heads!*

For us, that jolt of reality began when our first child, Tyler, was born. He was born with all the normal fanfare. We were juiced up on excitement, expectations, and unrealistic goals. Like most first-time parents, we were going to be different. Well, not just different—better. Our marriage and family would be a little slice of heaven on earth. Yes, older, wiser couples had warned us of the pitfalls, but we were convinced that their concerns revealed how they had missed the mark. Our marriage would be healthier, our kids more obedient, and life together blissful.

We shouldn't have been so surprised by reality. After all, our picture of the perfect marriage had already begun to crumble, and when kids came along, the crumbling not only continued, it accelerated! Maybe it was the first sleepless night when Tyler came home, followed by many more. Or maybe it was the endless rounds of breast-feeding. No matter what the cause, we quickly realized marriage *with kids* was going to be very different from what we had expected!

Then child number two came along. Not long after that, number three. Finally, with number four, we were calling it a family. We loved being parents, but we also found ourselves at times thoroughly outmatched, tired, sometimes irritable, short on income, but incredibly grateful for coffee—lots of it.

It is no wonder couples forget what a marriage is supposed to look like when kids come along. Nobody prepared us for kids wetting the bed in the middle of the night, throwing up in the car, crying uncontrollably because of growing pains, and fighting during dinner. We had no idea that children seem to come with previous training in how to interrupt, invade a conversation, or infiltrate a quiet moment of serenity! We never imagined that finishing a thought—let alone a conversation—would seem impossible. And we certainly never suspected the ridiculous cost of teenagers' shoes, braces, and well, just about everything else!

We have been married for more than seventeen years, and our four children—Tyler, Bella, Noah, and Sophia—are ages seven to fourteen. We love serving in ministry, spending time together as a family, reading, and drinking lots of coffee. And we still love each other! But nurturing our marriage in the midst of parenting hasn't been easy. The reality of life with children doesn't always match up with the rosy picture of family life we had envisioned.

Dreaming of Family

From an early age, I (*Ruth*) remember dreaming of getting married and having a large family. I had it all planned out and couldn't wait to have as many children as I could. What I envisioned was rosy and perfect, just like my grandma's house. There was only one problem: Grandma's kids no longer lived at home! When I visited, it was just me. No wonder it seemed so tranquil and lovely! Life with four kids doesn't match that vision I developed at Grandma's house.

My dream of having a large family coincided with an expectation that building that family would be fun . . . and easy! Instead, that expectation was shattered when I endured five miscarriages, one in between each of the births of our living children, then two more. It was like clockwork. I would have a child and then miscarry the next pregnancy. When I miscarried twice in a row after our youngest daughter, Sophia, was born, I knew I was done. My plan for a family with six children was not going to happen.

I also believed that raising a family would be filled with fun game nights, long dinners spent with meaningful conversations, and endless family time together. Little did I know at the time that sporting events and extracurricular activities would pull us in so many different directions. And sometimes conversations around the dinner table erupt into a sibling spat rather than a meaningful conversation. Imagine that! Although family time is something we enjoy, it doesn't just "happen." It is time we have to "fight for."

I (*Patrick*) grew up with two older sisters. My mom ran a successful home day care for more than forty years, so it felt as if I had about fifteen siblings. I've always loved kids and I shared Ruth's enthusiasm for having children—but I wasn't necessarily sold on having a huge family. I thought that being a father was all about playing catch in the backyard, going on bike rides, and watching Monday Night Football. Changing diapers? Not so much!

Obviously we had some differences in our dreams of what our family would be like. Ruth dreamed of a large, well-behaved brood, while I envisioned a smaller tribe that would fit into one motel room. We both thought having kids would be fun and personally fulfilling—and it is! But we learned that what *we* wanted in regards to having kids wasn't nearly as important as what God wanted. God created and loves the family, and he has a plan for the family that is far greater than our plan. It doesn't always look like it or feel like it, but God is doing something big through the family. Let's see what God's plan is and what he wants to accomplish through two parents raising their children together.

Shortly after God joined Adam and Eve in the garden, he gave them the very first commandment:

> Be fruitful and increase in number; fill the earth and subdue it. Rule over the fish in the sea and the birds in the sky and over every living creature that moves on the ground. (Genesis 1:28)

Who wouldn't want to obey this command? So we did. We got married and became fruitful! We became a couple with children.

Psalm 127:3 describes children as a "reward." In Hebrew, the word translated "reward" is *sakar*, which literally means a wage or payment. We all love to get paid. I have never met anyone who received a paycheck and felt as if it was a burden. The Bible is saying that the gift of children is like money paid out to someone who has empty pockets. It is a payment that we can receive joyfully and one that we must also handle wisely.

In God's good plan for marriage, children aren't just a gift for the benefit of one couple. God created the family—parents and their children—to have a greater purpose: to be instrumental in building and shaping civilization. God created the family because it's good for a man and a woman, good for kids, and good for the world. Families are good for a man and a woman because raising children forces them to mature, to consider other people's needs and desires alongside their own. Families are good for kids because they need the nurturing, protection, wisdom, discipline, and guidance of a man and a woman who love them deeply. And families are good for the world because families are the incubator of civilization where adults are formed who serve all of us in innumerable ways.

Just the Two of Us

Discuss with your spouse how your expectations of family life have affected your marriage.

- Before you had children, what expectations did you have about family life and raising children?
- How have those expectations been shattered by reality?
- How has raising children affected your marriage?
- How can understanding and focusing on God's purpose and perspective on parenting help to restore your marital relationship?

Kids Fulfill God's Purpose

Psalm 127 includes another description of children that we love. The psalm, which most scholars attribute to King Solomon, who was both a builder and a father, starts out describing the necessity (with the help of the Lord) of building and guarding a house and a city. The opening theme is that unless the Lord blesses our efforts to build, we "labor in vain." Although the psalm starts out describing building a house and watching over a city, the entire second half describes children:

> Children are a heritage from the LORD,
> offspring a reward from him.
> Like arrows in the hands of a warrior
> are children born in one's youth.
> Blessed is the man
> whose quiver is full of them.
> They will not be put to shame
> when they contend with their opponents
> in court. (Psalm 127:3–5)

Did you catch that second description of children? They are "like arrows in the hands of a warrior." Arrows and swords were two primary weapons of warfare in the ancient world. Although we no longer depend on our children to defend us from marauding neighboring tribes, as the Israelites did, we face other sorts of enemies, such as loneliness, loss of meaning, sickness, and old age. Godly children grown to adulthood help to protect us from the "slings and arrows of outrageous fortune"[1] and provide comfort in the face of life's trials. Even before they reach adulthood, children help us battle other intangible enemies, like cynicism, meaninglessness, and self-centeredness. Who can sneer at the world when gazing into a baby's first smile? Who can feel replaceable when a child's whole existence depends on you? And who can cling to selfish ambition and vain conceit when a child is tugging at your elbow, begging to play?

Our children bring us countless joys, which help us to engage in the spiritual battles we face personally and in our ministry. Tyler is our easygoing and gentle-hearted son. He

---

1. The phrase originates with William Shakespeare's *Hamlet*.

has a quiet confidence that causes him to be fearless. There isn't much he is afraid of doing or trying. Bella, who we affectionately call "our flower," is kind, with a heart that loves to give. She is always the first one to buy a gift or write a note. Noah has kept us laughing. He is quiet but always calculating what is going on. With his quick wit, he has a way of bringing laughter no matter what the circumstances are. And Sophia, she lives in a world of her own! She is content to play by herself. She has a vivid and creative imagination. She wakes up smiling and ready to take on the world. Each of our kids, in their own way, has taught us to be brave, kind, fun, and willing to dream. More than just changing our marriage, they have changed us—for the better.

We love the description of children being arrows because it reminds us that we are raising kids who will grow up to fulfill God's purpose by piercing the darkness of the world in which they live. In God's hands, our children will become weapons of truth, life, and light in a dark, broken, and hurting world.

We often overlook the truth that our families and kids are not only important to us as parents but they also are important to God. God is looking for a new generation to stand up and stand apart for his glory and for the good of the world. The future strength of our homes and cities depends on the kind of children we raise in our homes and release into the world. God's purpose and plan through marriage and family is to build, or rebuild, a city by first birthing and building the right kind of child. God has a plan and a vision for each couple and family. So we must be careful to not only see our marriage and kids as God does but to steward our marriage and family the way God wants us to.

The Mission in the Middle of the Mess

As amazing as it seems to us, God has designed the family to be one of his primary vehicles for passing on faith to the next generation. So amidst all of the messiness of life with kids, we have a mission. The good news is, the Bible doesn't leave us in the dark about what God desires or how to pass on faith to the next generation.

The Old Testament book of Deuteronomy contains one of the key passages of Scripture where God describes his purpose for parents to pass on their faith to their children. Through Moses, God shared the vision and instructed parents on how to be teachers of his Word. As Moses stood before the Israelite community, he said:

> Hear, O Israel: The LORD our God, the LORD is one. Love the LORD your God with all your heart and with all your soul and with all your strength. These commandments that I give you today are to be upon your hearts. Impress them on your children. Talk about them when you sit at home and when you walk along the road, when you lie down and when you get up. Tie them as symbols on your hands and bind them on your foreheads. Write them on the doorframes of your houses and on your gates. (Deuteronomy 6:4–9)

God's truth was to be at the center of every parent's life as they passed on faith to their children. They were even supposed to "write" the truth of God's Word on the doorframes of their homes. The Jewish people have taken this instruction seriously. Even today, thousands of years after Moses spoke these words, you will find in many Jewish homes a small wooden or metal box attached to the right doorframe at the entrance and on the right doorframe to every room. Inside is a mezuzah, a rolled piece of parchment or sheepskin with this passage and Deuteronomy 11:13–21 handwritten in Hebrew on it. The mezuzah serves as a constant reminder for parents that they are to faithfully live out God's truth and teach his Word to their children.

This short passage clarifies our mission as parents.

First, God commands parents to "impress" his commandments on their children (Deuteronomy 6:7). In Hebrew, the word means to "sharpen" and frequently describes the sharpening of a sword or arrow. The idea is that just as someone consistently whets, or sharpens, an object to make it useful and effective, parents are to faithfully "sharpen," or instruct, their children in God's words and ways.

Second, God instructs parents that their teaching isn't just transferring new information to their children. God desires parents to teach their children within the context of loving relationships in the classroom of life. This context provides the opportunity for children to not only learn God's Word but also grow to love God's Word and to put God's ways into practice in every part of life. Ultimately the goal of our teaching as parents is to disciple our children in the Christian faith so they will develop a personal relationship with Jesus.

What does this kind of daily discipleship look like in the Schwenk household?

First, we try to build spiritual habits into our lives so that we are continually reminded of our relationship with God. We intentionally talk about our own relationship with God. We share with our kids what God is teaching us and how it affects our family. When we sit down for a meal, we bow our heads and pray. When we head off on a road trip, we pray aloud for God's protection and blessing. At the end of the day, just before bed, we often gather for family devotions, Bible reading, discussion, and prayer. And when Sunday rolls around, we gather to worship with other believers. As our kids have gotten older, we have looked for ways to get them involved in serving at church.

Second, we try to stay alert and aware of God's work in our lives and the lives of our children. We recently moved to a new city to start a church. We celebrated with our kids when our home sold in just a few days, when God provided a perfect location for our new church to meet in, and when members of the core group who moved with us found new jobs. We love the outdoors. This past summer we spent a week in western Michigan. Our kids were begging me (*Patrick*) to go fishing. I prefer to just paddle around the lake. The fewer worms and fish I have to touch the better! But one morning we set our alarms early and headed out on the water to fish. We talked about God's beauty as we watched the sun come up. About his creativity as we saw different frogs and turtles.

Third, we find ways to teach spiritual life lessons as we go through the day. Through careful discipline we teach a toddler to share, a preschooler to tell the truth, a schoolchild to persevere in homework. Because we moved into a more diverse city and neighborhood, our kids have gained friends who are from different faiths. Even at a young age, they have an opportunity to be a good example of a Christian to someone of a different faith. Simply making new friends has been a way for us to teach them about making a difference in other people's lives.

God works through everyday people and in everyday circumstances to accomplish his purposes. Preparing our children, each of whom is a unique and valuable individual, to step into the future and fulfill their role as God's arrows in the world is a huge job. If you are feeling the whiplash effect in your marriage because of children, it means you are right where God wants you to be. After all, we are going to need him for this enormous task of living out his purpose and plan for marriage with kids.

While married life with children can be challenging, we have reason to hope and to be encouraged. There is a way forward, a way through, and a way beyond all of the craziness. God's Word has not changed. The promises of his Word still stand. Is being married with kids messy? Yes! Does God have a purpose and plan in the midst of it all? Of course he does! And do we enjoy taking part in this crazy, life-changing, impossible mission of parenting? Absolutely!

— 3 —

THE MISSING VOW

Love Your Spouse
with Kids in the House

A promise must be about things that I can do,
about actions: no one can promise to go on feeling
in a certain way.

C. S. Lewis, *Mere Christianity*

My (*Patrick's*) father passed away suddenly in 2010, just eight months short of what would have been fifty years of marriage to my mom. Not long afterward, my oldest sister gave his wedding ring to me. That gift reminds me how he sacrificially loved my mom for nearly five decades. That ring also brings to mind memories I have as a kid sitting on my father's lap, spinning that gold ring around his finger. It was nothing more to me at the time than jewelry. I would tug on it. Spin it. Hold it in the palm of my hand. Eventually I'd slip it on, where it would hang, obviously oversized for my tiny little fingers.

It never occurred to me until my wedding day, when Ruth slipped my own wedding ring onto my finger, that something so small could be so weighty. The ring immediately felt oversized. Not because it was too big for my adult finger, but because of how significant wearing a wedding ring is. It was going to take some growing to step into my new role as Ruth's husband. A bit panicked would be a good way of describing how I felt standing at the altar that day!

Now, as a pastor, I have the joy and privilege of officiating at many weddings. Sometimes it is hard for me to watch couples walk down the aisle after exchanging their vows. I know they are walking into the great unknown. I wonder if they, as I did on my wedding day, feel a bit panicked by the thought of what lies ahead. I wonder if in the future they will be faithful to the vows they have made to each other. I wonder what they will walk through and how they will respond when kids come along. Will they fight for, and not against, each other? Will they see their rings only as costly jewelry, or will they see them as a reminder of a sacred and costly calling to lay down their lives for each other? Will they walk down the aisle together *and* continue through life together?

I think of my father's wedding ring and imagine the day he and my mom stood at the altar on their wedding day. I expect they had their own picture of marriage—a vision probably not unlike yours or mine. They would exchange their rings. Say their vows. Declare their love. Say "I do." Then life would happen! They too would experience the crumbling, messiness, and goodness that marriage and children bring.

I am thankful for the encouragement the example of my parents' marriage and life provides. They didn't lose sight of God's purpose and intent of working toward a God-honoring marriage as they raised us. Of course, they didn't always love perfectly, but they lived faithfully. They did whatever was necessary to keep their vows to love each other in all of life.

The Missing Vow

The traditional wedding vows a couple make have been around for a while. They date back to the Church of England during the sixteenth century. These vows are a commitment about the couple's future together. These are not vows to feel a certain way, but are a promise, pledge, or declaration of intent to behave in a certain way toward each other:

> I take you to be my wife (husband),
> To have and to hold,
> From this day forward,
> For better, for worse,
> For richer, for poorer,
> In sickness and in health,
> To love and to cherish,
> 'Til death do us part.

These are enormous vows! They encompass God's purpose and plan for marriage. They are selfless, costly, sacrificial, committed, and one-another-centered vows. They express the heart of God for a man and a woman as they enter into the sacred covenant of marriage.

However, there is one problem. There is a missing vow—and it's a big one! It is the vow to love your spouse with kids in the house.

The missing vow has to do with our commitment to love each other when we transition from marriage as a couple to marriage with children. Without this vow, we lack the complete picture of God's vision for marriage and family. Without this vow, we are quite comfortable living a child-centered or me-centered marriage. It comes naturally to us! So we need this vow to remind us that God has something more—a God-centered marriage and family—for us. That kind of marriage requires making a vow to go on loving each other with kids in the house.

Why Is the Missing Vow So Important?

Marriage is both a blessing we receive and a battle we fight for in love, commitment, sacrifice, and grace. The challenge in marriage is not how it starts, but how it continues, grows, matures, and flourishes over time. The transition from marriage to family creates a whole new set of complexities and threats to the marriage relationship that can make it difficult to keep our marriage vows. Suddenly the relationship is no longer about pleasing each other; it now includes the responsibility of caring for other needy (and sinful) members of the family! So the work of keeping the husband-wife relationship a priority requires a lot of effort.

It might sound strange, but one of the greatest challenges we face in order to live out the missing vow is our desire to be great parents. Most couples who have children have a sincere desire to be really good parents. Raising and releasing kids to love God and love the world requires an immense amount of time, energy, work, and prayer! So we pour ourselves into it with everything we've got. After all, what could be so bad about wanting to be great parents?

The Child-Centered Marriage

The problem arises when our desire to be great parents overshadows our desire to have a great marriage. Out of our desire to raise kids the right way, our love for each other gets kicked to the curb. Not intentionally, of course. It just happens. The effects are seldom seen or noticed immediately, but they can eventually grow into significant problems:

- A couple's needs are neglected.
- Intimacy dwindles.
- Romance cools.
- Conflicts go unresolved.
- Meaningful communication becomes infrequent or nonexistent.
- Attention and affection shift from spouse to child.
- Financial decisions are dominated by the child's needs and wants.

All of these indicate that a couple is moving into the arena of being too child centered. The child's needs and concerns are being met at the expense of a once healthy and God-honoring marriage. This is completely normal! It is to be expected during times of transition, but it is not to become a way of life.

In our own marriage, we experienced all of the challenges of moving from married to married with kids. We loved being parents. We did Pizza Nights because Tyler loves to eat. We did

Signs of a Child-Centered Marriage

When kids come along, every couple struggles to maintain God's purpose and plan for their marriage. The following assessment can help you determine if your marriage and family are in danger of being child centered:

1. Do you often feel too busy, overcommitted, or worn out because of your child's activities?

2. Do you ever feel as if your children have too few responsibilities because you and your spouse are doing it all?

3. Do you and your spouse struggle to find time for date nights (at least twice a month) because of your child's activities?

4. Do the two of you find it difficult to make time to go away for a weekend (without the kids) because of your children's schedules?

5. Has your physical intimacy lost some of the passion and romance because you have given your all to your children's priorities to the extent that you feel too tired, busy, distracted, or just not interested in engaging with your spouse?

6. Do you ever feel that your needs and desires are neglected because of the attention your spouse gives to your child?

7. Do you ever feel surrounded by family but lonely in your marriage?

8. Do you ever feel as if most of your communication with your spouse is about the kids instead of about each other?

9. Have you not gone on family vacations because of a child's sport or other activity?

10. Do you ever feel as if your child's wants and desires, instead of you and your spouse, are charting the course for your family?

If you answered yes to five or more questions, you are experiencing a child-centered marriage and family. If you answered yes to three or four questions, you are in danger of becoming a child-centered marriage and family.

Sports Nights because Noah is our little competitor. And we did Movie Nights because Sophia and Bella love a great story. We even tried a few Adventure Nights (campouts in the back-yard), which didn't go so well! In all of the fun of being parents, we needed the reminder that it was okay to continue being great lovers. We haven't stopped doing some of these fun things as a family, but we have intentionally built in time for just the two of us. It's possible to have a great family and a great marriage.

This is where the missing vow—our commitment to continue to love our spouse when we have kids in the house— comes into play. When we dig a little deeper into how we function in everyday life, we may find some normal (but not always good) motivating factors that can lead any couple into trouble. Let's take a look at these areas and renew our com-mitment to put love for our kids *and* our spouse each in its rightful place.

Many of us want to be great parents because we are fearful of getting it wrong. We genuinely want our kids to be healthy and happy as they grow up. But fear can lead us to believe that we need to be perfect parents. We can become so concerned and consumed about not doing everything right that parenting becomes everything to us. Like a giant vacuum, our fear of failing as parents sucks the energy and excitement out of our marriage!

Sometimes we think that being great parents means we must give our kids everything we didn't have growing up. We want to do what we can to provide for our children and set them up for success when they leave home. On the surface, giving our kids the best of everything sounds noble, but it isn't always the best for them. This is especially true if the pursuit of giving them the best creates distance between a husband and a wife. This distance can creep in if we are engaged in too many activities or continually justify extra hours at work for the sake of our kids. An expensive education, trendy clothes, training or coaching in specific activities, or a certain quality of lifestyle may all be good things. But we have to consider our motivation. If we feel driven to provide certain things in order to right what we felt our parents got wrong, it can drive a wedge between a husband and a wife.

Finally, our desire to be great parents may be driven by what our culture says our kids should have rather than by what God says they should have. Just like a bunch of middle schoolers who do what the crowd is doing, we can blindly follow what our culture says is normal. This might be in the area of education, clothing, experiences, and activities. Trying to measure up to what others are doing around us can lead us to place too much emphasis on our parenting and not enough on our marriage.

The Me-Centered Marriage

Having a child-centered marriage isn't the only threat to living out the vow to love your spouse with kids in the house. The other greatest threat to living out this missing vow is "me"!

I (*Patrick*) met with a couple in the middle of trying to manage their marriage with kids in the house. The husband looked at me and said, "It's just so hard! I want to come home and enjoy some peace and quiet." Who doesn't want that? The problem was, he always wanted peace and quiet. Over time, his continued desire and demand for an easier road was becoming an excuse for avoiding the hard work of loving his wife.

Another couple I met with had fallen on hard times, not financially, but relationally. The couple had a rocky relationship. The wife's expectations for marriage and family were so high that not even Dr. Phil could have met them. Her husband was trying, but her ideal picture was too demanding for anyone in the real world to achieve. It was not God's picture she was chasing after; it was her own.

We understand these emotional needs and desires. My (*Patrick's*) office is only five minutes from our house. While the short commute might be good for saving money on gas, sometimes it's not nearly enough time to decompress after a long day! There are plenty of days when I think, *It would be really nice to just go in the house and hop on the computer, go for a run, take a nap, or just veg out!* Then I remember I am driving a minivan for a reason. I am married. I am a husband and a father. So much for "me" time!

I (*Ruth*) have to admit that it's easy to just want to hand the kids off to Patrick the second he walks in the door. I want to instantly enlist him to help with letting the dogs out, helping a child with homework, finishing dinner, or running to the grocery store. After a long day of my own, I wouldn't mind time to myself either! After all, I'd rather be shopping. Let the chef and maid take care of things! Then I remember I am married. I am a wife and a mother, and we don't have a chef or a maid.

We all feel the challenge of trying to have a God-honoring marriage and family. Because of the personal sacrifices we make for our spouse and children, we may feel we "deserve" something more for ourselves. But one of the greatest threats to experiencing God's plan and purpose for marriage and family is our own selfishness. We can become too me-centered. As a result we may:

- neglect responsibilities because we feel we've done enough;
- disengage emotionally or physically—check out when we should be checking in;
- become too busy at work for meaningful time with our spouse or family;
- base all our decisions on what we want instead of what is best or right for our spouse;
- become too demanding or controlling—insisting that things be done our way and in our time;
- act with pride, as if we are always right;
- lack compassion and understanding when the unexpected happens.

The threat of a child-centered marriage or a me-centered marriage can lead a marriage and family astray. This can cause us to live out of balance and out of sync with God's vision. His picture of marriage and family can become distorted. To fully enjoy what he has given us, we have to come back to what he wants.

Just the *Two* of Us

Take some time to talk about how focusing more on a God-centered marriage, instead of a child-centered or me-centered marriage, could make your relationship stronger and more healthy.

- What good things have we made a priority for our kids that might not be good for us as a couple?
- What can we do to pay better attention to our marriage and balance that priority?
- In what ways are we each sometimes me-centered? How can we gently prod each other away from selfish behavior?

Selfless Lovers

After being gone for a weekend speaking at a mom's conference, I (*Ruth*) arrived safely on the ground at our nearest airport. Still an hour and a half from home, I began to dread the responsibilities awaiting me. *There's probably loads of laundry waiting*, I thought. *I wonder if anyone has done the dishes? Did anyone think to feed the fish?* On and on I played the tape in my head of what I would walk into. Much to my surprise (sorry, honey), I was wrong. When I got home the house was clean, laundry was done, fish were alive, and the kids were even bathed!

I (*Patrick*) wish I was always this much of a servant. On this occasion, I was on my game!

We must become selfless lovers of each other if we are to be successful in living out the missing vow. God intended for us to have both a God-honoring marriage and a God-honoring family. Both are possible, but they are impossible without a foundation of selfless and sacrificial love. Jesus is our ultimate example of how to live out a life of sacrificial love.

> In your relationships with one another, have the same mindset as Christ Jesus:
>
> > Who, being in very nature God,
> > > did not consider equality with God something
> > > to be used to his own advantage;
> > rather, he made himself nothing
> > > by taking the very nature of a servant,
> > > being made in human likeness.
> > And being found in appearance as a man,
> > > he humbled himself
> > > by becoming obedient to death—
> > > > even death on a cross! (Philippians 2:5–8)

Jesus was a selfless lover. He sacrificed power, position, and pleasure to move in our direction. He gave us what we did not deserve. He did for us what we could never do for ourselves. In Christ, God selflessly and sacrificially served us to save us, and he commanded us to follow in his footsteps as we humbly love and serve one another. We are to be Christ centered so that we do not become too child centered or me-centered.

The missing vow—to love your spouse with kids in the

house—fulfills God's intent, hope, and vision for marriage and family. With all of the changes and challenges that children bring to life, it is critical that we not neglect the husband-wife relationship. We need the friendship and companionship of the spouse God gave to us. Our spouse helps lighten the heavy responsibility kids bring into our marriage. While parenting is full of self-sacrifice and costly love, there is also room to make our marriage, our husband-wife relationship, a priority.

Just recently, we were telling our kids that we were going out for dinner. "Dad is taking your mom out for a romantic dinner," I told our oldest son. "We are going out to get away," I added.

"Get away from us?" he asked, half joking and half serious.

"Exactly!" I said.

One of the greatest gifts we can give our kids is a healthy, loving, and God-honoring marriage. Children will join us on the journey, but we have to be careful that they don't come between us on this journey.

— 4 —

FANNING THE FLAMES

Sex with Your Spouse with Kids in the House

Pleasure is God's idea, and God is the devil's Enemy. The devil actually hates pleasure, because he hates the God of pleasure.
Ben Patterson, *Sex and the Supremacy of Christ*

"So, *is* there sex after kids?" we asked some friends. Ruth was close to giving birth to our firstborn, and this was an important question. We had heard the horror stories about romance after kids. We needed answers. Or at least I (*Patrick*) needed answers.

How could the very thing that brought these kids into the world be lost once they arrived? I wondered. It was understandable from a physical perspective to need some recovery time after childbirth. But the stories of no sex for an extended time—stories of tired moms, diminished sex drives, limited privacy, and loss of spontaneity in the bedroom—that got my attention. As a man, husband, and father, I was concerned.

I (*Ruth*) wasn't that worried about it. I was having my first child, and all I could think about was caring for him. *Of course I'll still spend plenty of time with my husband in the bedroom*, I thought. *What's the big deal?* I let it pass as a fleeting thought, convinced that everything would remain the same.

Boy, was I wrong! I was in no way prepared for how my body felt physically and how I felt emotionally after giving birth.

Our Sex Life Has . . . Changed

The answer to the question we posed to our friends, of course, is yes. There is sex after kids. But if you are like most couples, romance in general is different after kids enter the picture. The early years of marriage with kids were tough.

As a guy, I (*Patrick*) wasn't overly sensitive to the fact that a seven-pound human being had passed out of Ruth's body. Lacking wisdom and full of selfishness, I was oblivious to even the physical changes caused by having kids.

For me (*Ruth*), sex and romance became more of an afterthought. It wasn't that I didn't love and want to be with my husband; I was just exhausted. With the constant pull and tug of parenting, sex at the end of the day sometimes seemed too much. I wasn't always sensitive to my husband's need.

We both lacked wisdom. Nothing had changed for me (*Patrick*). Everything had changed for me (*Ruth*). We had to learn to reengage and cultivate a healthy life of romance. By God's grace, a lot of trial and error, lots of communication, and added maturity, we have a better sex life now than ever. But there is no doubt that it takes intentional effort, laughter, and lots of humility to create a healthy sex life with kids in the house. We still have to work at it.

We used to live in a 1920s-era home. We loved everything about that house except one thing. Our bedroom door didn't lock. With kids who shared rooms directly across the hall from us, we had to practically remodel our bedroom just to keep the door closed!

Here was the drill. We first had to move the bedside table in front of the bedroom door. The lamp that sat on this table had a short cord, so it had to either be unplugged and moved with the table or relocated to the floor. Because the table was not terribly heavy, we then had to wedge a plastic laundry basket (preferably loaded with clothes for extra weight) securely against the table. Finally, a large recliner had to be carried across the room. All of this had to be done in near silence so as not to waken the kids or cause undue concern that we were moving out. It wasn't terribly romantic, but it was what we had to do during that season of life to have some privacy and to keep our passion a priority.

Why did we go to all that trouble? For two reasons: First, we like sex and wanted to. Second, we valued our relationship and needed to.

Sex—A Good Gift to Be Enjoyed

Sex is an important part of a healthy marriage. It joins a man and a woman together unlike any other experience. We learn at the very beginning of the Bible that our sexuality is a good gift from God. In the sexual experience, a husband and wife can be completely free and vulnerable to enjoy each other.

God declared everything he created, including marriage and sexuality, to be good. His desire for marriage, as summarized in Genesis 2:24, was for a man and a woman to be joined together, build a family, and thoroughly enjoy it: "That is why a man leaves his father and mother and is united to his wife, and they become one flesh."

God in his very nature is full of joy, pleasure, intimacy, and creativity. Our experience of sex, when it brings about joy and oneness, gives us a picture of the joy and intimacy that is ours in Christ for all eternity. As is true with every gift God gives, he wants us to steward it wisely. God wants us to enjoy the pleasure and intimacy of sex, but it should always be in its proper place—never becoming more important to us than loving God and loving each other, and never becoming less than it should be.

We are responsible to not only enjoy but also protect and preserve the gift of sex throughout our married life. In Mark 10:6–9, the Bible says that a husband and wife should "let no one separate" them. This means we need to protect our intimacy from invaders! We generally think this refers to marital unfaithfulness, the breaking of our covenant vows with someone other than our spouse. But there's another consideration. If we are not careful, our own offspring can come between us and diminish our intimacy.

This is the tricky part about keeping marriage a priority relationship with kids in the house. We don't generally think of our children as potential threats. We know we need to guard the fidelity of our relationship with our spouse from another man or another woman. Rarely do we think that our marriage needs to be protected from our own flesh and blood. But it does—especially if we want to keep our relational and physical intimacy alive.

It is no secret that our enjoyment of and engagement in sex face new challenges when kids come along. This is especially true during the early years of having children. This season of life, when sex may be painful, less frequent, or harder work, can wreak havoc on our sex life. It requires keeping our understanding of sex in proper balance.

Because kids have an impact on a couple's romance, we have to be careful to not let parenting deprive our marriage of passion. God has given us sex for our benefit, enjoyment, and intimacy. While we may be tempted to neglect this gift, a healthy marriage is intent on keeping passion a priority by fanning the flames.

Having children doesn't mean we have to sacrifice the romance we once had. Kids in the house require an adjustment to romance, but it doesn't have to mean the absence of romance.

"Dad, What Is Song of Songs?"

One of our kids inadvertently reminded us recently of how much the Bible has to say about the gift of romance. In fact, we had to censor their Bible reading after their discovery!

On a Friday night we loaded our tribe into the minivan and headed out to eat. Our destination was about an hour away, so the kids brought books and magazines to occupy their time on the drive. Our oldest daughter brought her Bible.

We are thrilled that our children are at an age when they can and want to read the Bible on their own. So we were feeling pretty good that she had brought her Bible to read. We sailed down the highway with a sense of joy and accomplishment. Twenty minutes into our ride and our daughter's reading, we heard the question. We asked her to repeat it just to be sure, and yes, we heard it right the first time.

"What is Song of Songs?" she asked.

We are both Moody Bible Institute grads, so we knew exactly what Songs of Songs is. Trying to buy some time, wishing I (*Patrick*) could "phone a friend," I nervously fumbled for the right words. "What was that, pumpkin?"

"What is Songs of Songs?" she asked again.

"It's a book in the Old Testament," I said. "You know, it's kind of . . . ah . . . like a love song, or poem . . . between a husband and a wife, of course. Why?" (Yikes!) We both knew the answer to why she was asking but didn't want to overreact.

"Well, that's awkward," she said.

"Yes, yes, it is. Ummm, why don't you just stick to the New Testament right now?"

For the next forty minutes, I kept glancing in the rearview mirror to make sure she was staying out of Solomon's steamy love poem! Who knew we'd have to censor our kids' Bible reading!

This interaction with our daughter is a reminder of how much the Bible has to say about romance. Just look at some of the intimate language found in the Song of Songs:

> Let him kiss me with the kisses of his mouth —
> for your love is more delightful than wine. (1:1)
> How beautiful you are, my darling!
> Oh, how beautiful!
> Your eyes are doves.

How handsome you are, my beloved!
    Oh, how charming!
    And our bed is verdant. (1:15–16)
Strengthen me with raisins,
    refresh me with apples,
    for I am faint with love.
His left arm is under my head,
    and his right arm embraces me. (2:5–6)
How beautiful you are and how pleasing,
    my love, with your delights!
Your stature is like that of the palm,
    and your breasts like clusters of fruit. (7:6–7)

I grew up in church as a pastor's kid and had no idea until I was in college that such language was in the Bible! Song of Songs is a great celebration of the love between a husband and a wife. It is a beautiful, and at times graphic, demonstration of God's intention for marriage. Who knew? Sex was God's idea, his gift to us. When a couple enter into romance and sex on God's terms, sex is an incredible blessing to be enjoyed. Let's make sure we guard and grow our romance, even with kids in the house.

Things Have Changed (But Not Forever)

It always feels a little uncomfortable when your doctor talks to you about sex. But we were especially interested on this occasion. The doctor was telling us what to expect after childbirth. I (*Ruth*) had already told Patrick it would be at least six weeks, maybe longer, before we could have sex. Of course, he didn't believe me. Or at least he was in denial. Then the doctor broke the news.

I looked at Patrick and refrained from blurting out, "I told you so!"

If you are a mom with young children and you are still in the season of childbirth, then sex and romantic feelings may be the furthest things from your mind. All you want to do at the end of the day is bury your head in a pillow and enjoy the silence and the sleeping. The last thing you want is more activity. Six weeks or not, you don't want anyone, including your husband, touching your body—especially not your breasts!

As a guy, I (*Patrick*) completely missed the memo on the effects of childbirth on a woman's body. Everything changes after children, and I had to learn this the hard way. I had no idea that real hormonal and biological changes were taking place. Like a lot of guys, I took Ruth's lack of interest personally. I assumed something was wrong with me. I also thought something was not only different but really wrong with her.

Many of our fights during those years stemmed from my not understanding that this season of a new mom's life is very difficult. There were no changes in my body. I could not comprehend what was going on in her body.

Dr. John Gartner notes the significance of this hormonal change in women after having children. He writes, "The abrupt change in sexual connection between partners is hormonally influenced. Throughout the nursing years, prolactin production depresses the sex hormones estrogen and testosterone, biologically encouraging women to de-emphasize mating and focus energy on keeping their newborn alive. Further, breastfeeding stimulates the bonding hormone oxytocin;

it prompts a shift in attention toward baby and away from husband."[1]

Yes, there was a lot going on in my (*Ruth's*) body. Not only was I tired, emotional, and angry all at the same time, but I felt like a whale washed up on shore. This was a hard time for me. I really wish someone had told me that those years were just a season. Pregnancy and childbirth, newborns and toddlers are all just part of a season, and for many of us that season is very short.

If you find this season difficult for your sex life, don't lose heart. I (*Patrick*) had to understand that this season is full of changes for the woman. For me this meant learning to be patient, gracious, and understanding. For me (*Ruth*), I had to learn that although this season was different, our romance and intimacy could not be neglected. Realizing that we had different needs and desires during this challenging season did not give me an excuse to withhold or neglect our physical intimacy.

Dating: Time Away for Two

We remember well our first date as parents. It was the first time we had been out since our oldest son, Tyler, was born nearly a year earlier. Although we were at times exhausted from nonstop parenting, sleep deprivation, and not enough adult stimulation, we really loved being with our son. But we finally made time to go out. Technically, we were forced to go out. Good friends kindly, but sternly, informed us that we

---

1. John Gartner and Henry Leutwyler, "Child-ol'-a-try," *Psychology Today* (August 2014): 59–60.

would be leaving our son, our only son, the one we loved, at their house for the evening.

Our only responsibility was to go on a date. We didn't totally understand their persistence at the time, but we soon came to appreciate their wisdom. They understood the need for mom and dad to get away, alone, as husband and wife.

For close to a year we had been grinding out the grins, giggles, and utter terror of being responsible for a human being in diapers. We hadn't really talked about it, but we secretly resigned ourselves to a new reality that revolved around our child. Dates were a thing of the past (or so we thought). Alone time? There was none.

And so we went out, reluctantly. It might have been the shortest date in history. Both of us lasted about an hour without our child. We desperately needed the time away, but we were anxious to get back. After all, we were his parents. What if he bonded too much with our friends? Was he suffering from separation anxiety? Frightened? Hungry? Would he still recognize our voices? We scarfed down our food, skipped the movie, and went back to pick him up.

Our concerns were a bit inflated. As new parents, we were consumed with being the best parents. We were overly focused on trying to do everything right—so much so we couldn't even enjoy time away without the kiddo occupying our every thought and conversation! It is a good thing to want to parent well, but not if it interferes with cultivating a healthy marriage where intimacy is alive and growing. A healthy marriage is one of the greatest gifts we can give our children.

As a pastor, I (*Patrick*) do some marriage counseling. I almost always ask, "When was the last time you were out on a date?" And I am always surprised by how infrequently couples have time alone together. These are answers I typically hear:

- "Never."
- "I can't tell you the last time we've been out."
- "We haven't been out since we got married."
- "Last year!"

Excuses for not spending time alone together are usually predictable and understandable—not enough time, too expensive, we never schedule it.

We understand the pressures and complications, but they don't change the need to keep the marriage alive and healthy. We need to give ourselves permission to get away and get alone—together.

Although our first attempt at dating after kids didn't go so well, we have since made date nights a must in our schedule. When our kids were very young and finances were tight, it took a lot of effort and planning. One thing that worked was cooperating with other couples in a similar situation. We took turns watching each other's kids on date nights. This provided a free night of babysitting so that each couple could go out without the added cost of paying a babysitter.

Every couple is different and has to figure out what works best for them. We still try to go out at least twice a month just by ourselves. If possible, we plan a weekend away once a year for just the two of us. We are always amazed by how recharged and refreshed we are from our time away. Every couple needs to feed and nurture their marriage, so we encourage you to get away and get alone. Your love life needs it!

Just the *Two* of Us

There are many ways a husband and wife can cultivate a healthier romantic life. Take some time for just the two of you to explore ways to keep your romantic love alive.

- Identify one or two changes that could make a positive impact on your romance right now.
- What can you and your spouse do to make physical intimacy more of a priority in life?
- What can you do that will cause your spouse to feel more desired and pursued by you?

Scheduling Sex

Speaking of nurturing your love life, how does this romantic encounter sound?

"So, apparently you are just going to bed then?" I (*Patrick*) asked. I didn't give Ruth time to answer. I rolled over, feeling a bit rejected and angry.

"Well, I don't have to," Ruth said. "I am exhausted and thought you were just going to bed," she added.

"Never mind," I said.

"Oh, brother." Ruth sighed.

By this time, my romantic feelings were long gone. My immature response and my shattered expectations ensured there would be no romance between the two of us.

We had had a long day. Work, meetings, parenting, and

soccer games. I (*Patrick*) thought a perfect end to a long day was a little romance. Ruth thought a perfect end to a busy day was some sleep. We had very different expectations for what was on the schedule that night! So we went to bed mad.

It may not sound terribly romantic, but sometimes we need to schedule time for sex. Just because we have to plan for it doesn't mean we won't still enjoy it. Think back to when you were dating before marriage. Chances are you scheduled dates well in advance and looked forward to those nights with great expectation. You thought about what you were going to wear, where you would eat, and what you would talk about. Sex "dates" can be full of thoughtful planning and anticipation too.

Parenting packs a calendar quickly. It is very helpful when a couple share an understanding of which times are most desirable for having sex. A schedule takes the potential disappointment of unmet expectations out of the mix. The conflicts that start because one of us thought we were going to sleep and the other thought we were having sex go away.

Some couples schedule "quickies" several times a week, knowing that during the week their time together is limited. On the weekend, they pick a night for a lengthier romantic encounter that may include more kissing, foreplay, music, even candles. They can devote more time to one another because they don't feel the pressure of activities or the need to get up and go to work the next morning.

Every couple is different. You need to decide what works best for you. Whatever you do, you shouldn't compare your normal with what is normal for another couple. The important thing is to carve out time and space to engage romantically with each other.

Keep Boredom out of the Bedroom

Having a healthy sex life takes plenty of exploring, which is where the fun comes in. Many couples, especially with kids in the house, settle into an unhealthy rut in their romance. Sex is always done at the same time, in the same place, in the same way. The very act that is meant to bring incredible pleasure and intimacy can become about as interesting as brushing your teeth (that may be a little bit of an exaggeration). But be aware that, as with any new experience, there is a learning curve.

"What are you doing?" Ruth asked.

"Ummm, does that not feel good?" I sheepishly responded.

"Not even close!"

I (*Patrick*) was defeated and deflated. I was tired of having sex the same way all the time. So I thought I'd spice things up and go for something different. Different was right! Back to the drawing board!

We don't enter marriage and the bedroom having it all figured out. We had to learn how to drive a car. It will take time to figure out sex. So don't be afraid to talk to each other. There is no shame in working together to communicate about what works and what feels good. A couple's knowledge of each other should extend into the bedroom. Learning what pleases each other takes time, humility, and communication.

The point is, we should guard against letting boredom settle into our bedroom. Get creative. Read a book together. Try out new positions. Schedule a different time of day. Switch rooms. Do something different to spice things up!

Duty and Desire

Many men and women express and experience concern about their "duty" to each other. A husband and wife can go through seasons of life when physical intimacy no longer feels like the beautiful and enjoyable gift God intended it to be. So what can we do when duty replaces desire and sex feels like more of a chore than a gift?

While there is no formula or timeline for a solution, there are ways to help us get through a time of feeling less than passionate in the bedroom:

- Try something new or different. Boredom in the bedroom can leave a husband or a wife feeling less desire and more duty.

- Communicate what is pleasurable and what is not. Don't be afraid to talk with your spouse about what works and what doesn't.

- Get more rest. Stress, busyness, and physical or emotional exhaustion can suck the sizzle out of romance if we're not careful.

- Exercise. Working out is not easy for everyone, but it can improve energy, mood, and even our sex drive.

- Finally, be careful of depriving each other, even if the desire isn't always there (1 Corinthians 7:3–5).

Don't Stop Pursuing Each Other

As a marriage relationship progresses and time goes by, the temptation to stop pursuing our spouse is likely to set in. When kids come along, it is easy to stop trying. A husband and wife may sink into survival mode, forgetting all about pursuing each other or remaining attractive to each other. Both the husband and the wife can be guilty of letting themselves (and their relationship) go.

Please don't misunderstand. We're not pushing for a husband or wife to strive for an impossible standard of perfection. This is real life! Things begin to become routine and mundane. We forget that we should be our spouse's biggest fan. We get sloppy in expressing ongoing affection for our spouse. What we are saying is that a husband or a wife should never stop trying!

Each of us needs affirmation to feel loved and pursued. As a wife, I (*Ruth*) need to tell my husband I love him. I need to let him know that he looks nice, he's a good dad, that I appreciate his hard work. As a husband, I (*Patrick*) have to tell my wife how much I appreciate her. I need to make sure I am not taking her for granted or allowing her to feel starved emotionally or relationally. I need to tell her she is beautiful and that I notice her. She wants to know I still want her.

We need to pursue each other with more than just words. A gentle touch, a kiss good-bye or hello, an affectionate hug, and a lingering glance all show affection. As we are busy living life with kids in the house, we can continue to express our desire for each other in the language of affection. Physical affection fuels our desire to be together, even outside the bedroom.

Nothing is more destructive to a healthy and intimate

relationship than one spouse failing to pursue the other. That is why I (*Ruth*) want to be a wife who keeps pursuing my husband, not because I fear losing him but because I love him and deeply desire him. I don't want him to doubt that—ever. And I (*Patrick*) want to be a husband who keeps pursuing my wife so that she feels treasured, cared for, and beautiful. Pursuing each other is part of what it means to love our spouse with kids in the house.

— 5 —

PARENTING TOGETHER, NOT SEPARATELY

Many marriages would be better if the husband and wife clearly understood that they are on the same side.

Zig Ziglar

atrick owns very few pairs of dress pants. In fact, the gray pair he chose the day of his final interview for a senior pastor position were what you might call his "lucky" pants—dressy but casual pants he had worn for years. He always said they were the perfect fit. They had been faithful during our college years, our wedding reception, numerous funerals and weddings, and now, a huge interview.

The night was to be a "meet and greet" with the core group of the church. From 2:00 to 8:00 p.m., we were expected to mix and mingle with about eighty to a hundred leaders, volunteers, staff, and members. The former pastor of twenty-five years and the elders were already present and waiting to greet us as soon as we entered the home of the chairman of the elder board. Make it through this gathering and the job was his. This was big!

After about an hour's drive, we pulled up to the home and briskly walked up the front walk. I was trailing behind Patrick, and as we walked something caught my eye. Not only was this third and final interview big, so was the gaping split by the back pocket of Patrick's "lucky" pants! Not only that, it got larger with every step he took. The split was so big you could see through his pants to his underwear. The discovery came a little too late.

I tried not to sound too alarmed as I leaned forward and whispered, "Honey, I need to tell you something, but there isn't anything you can do about it right now. You have a huge hole in the back of your pants. I can see your underwear."

No sooner had those words come out of my mouth than the front door swung open. As we were warmly welcomed in, I saw Patrick reach back to verify my observation. We were all smiles, pretending that everything was fine and dandy, when the truth was we were filled with a sudden onset of fear and trembling.

For close to six hours we worked together like a well-synchronized ice-skating couple. Whenever Patrick moved, I followed. Knowing that he was "exposed," Patrick did everything in his power to stay close to me or keep his back to a wall, which proved to be very difficult in a room with fifty to a hundred people. We managed to keep in step, staying close with every turn and conversation. By God's grace, and a lot of effort, we managed to get through the night. Perhaps an even greater miracle was that the church offered Patrick the job later that week!

There have been countless times since then when we have had to function together as a team, but that night ranks close to the top! We laugh about it now, but at the time, it was horrifying. Together, we faced the challenge and succeeded.

The challenge in keeping our missing vow with kids in the house requires a lot of working together too. Kids quickly expose our weaknesses. Living out God's plan and purposes in marriage and family requires that we come alongside each other to parent as a well-synchronized team.

It Takes Two

Parenting is not just one spouse's responsibility. It takes two to bring children into the world, and it takes two to bring them up in the world. A husband and wife need to envision the same goal, have the same priorities, and be united in training and discipline. This doesn't always happen. A friend said to us recently, "We'd have a great marriage if we didn't have kids." Their good marriage had turned into a grind with kids. Differences in parenting were driving our friends apart.

When a husband and a wife are divided on parenting, it can be the source of tremendous conflict in the marriage. And we will have our differences. We were raised in different families, so we come into marriage and parenting with different expectations, preferences, styles, and philosophies. Maybe one spouse thinks children need a strict and disciplined environment, while the other thinks a child needs a more loving, grace-filled, and affectionate environment. Some couples disagree on who should do what. Perhaps one spouse was raised in a home where both parents worked outside of the home, so housework and parenting were shared responsibilities. The other spouse may have come from a home where the mom stayed at home and did most, if not all, of the housework and parenting. Personality differences can also play into parenting challenges. For instance, an extroverted parent might want to force a shy child into social situations, whereas an introverted parent might support that child's desire for just a few close friends.

In our own journey in parenthood, we discovered our expectations and discipline styles were very different. I (*Patrick*) was more of the disciplinarian. Early in our family years, I tended to have unrealistic expectations for our kids. I was too strict. Ruth was far more gentle and patient. While it has been hard at times, we have learned to humbly listen to each other. Ruth's parenting strengths have helped me to be far more understanding and aware of my weaknesses. Our differences have worked to balance each other out.

With such great differences, a healthy and vibrant marriage is possible only if we see our parenting as one job made for two. We need to recognize our expectations and differences and discover the best ways to support and serve each other. Maybe one is better at managing the minutia of family life—calendars and car pools and parent-teacher conferences—while the other is better at overseeing messy fun like baking cookies or carving pumpkins. Together, by God's grace, we can tackle the challenges of life with kids. Especially during the parenting years, a good marriage requires that we keep in step with each other—never too far ahead and never too far behind.

Let's Talk about Celebrating the Differences

Every couple brings to parenting different expectations, philosophies, approaches, and personalities. Those differences can be a source of conflict. But when viewed another way, they can greatly enrich our parenting and increase our gratitude for each other and what we each bring to the task of parenting. Use the questions that follow as discussion points to identify and celebrate your differences.

- What are your main parenting differences?
- In what areas of parenting are you each weakest? How can your spouse help you or balance you in that area?
- In what areas of parenting are you each strongest? How can you use that strength to help your spouse?

Remember, parenting is a huge job. Instead of grumbling about what your spouse does not do well as a parent, look for what you each contribute—and celebrate those gems!

It's Not Good to Parent Alone

God did not design us to do life alone. This is especially clear in Genesis 2:18, where "The LORD God said, 'It is not good for the man to be alone. I will make a helper suitable for him.'" So, out of Adam's side, God created Eve, a kindred spirit who would be his companion and soul mate.

Furthermore, God did not create us to be parents who fly solo. God made us to be a unified team. Through the sacred bond of marriage, that intimate companionship where two people become one flesh, a man and woman—together—are to live out God's command to "be fruitful and increase in number" (Genesis 1:28) by building a family for his purposes. That mission is something they could not possibly do alone.

Although a couple may be on the same page when it comes to marriage, it is easy to overlook the importance of our interdependence when it comes to parenting. Marriage with kids in the house takes two—a husband and wife who are deeply committed to each other and to the same goals, priorities, and vision for the way they parent their kids.

I (*Patrick*) will admit I was a little late to the game when it came to parenting. I played a small but enjoyable part in bringing our children into the world. After conception, parenting wasn't on my mind.

While I went about life as if nothing had changed, Ruth began creating a unique bond with the human being growing inside of her. Morning sickness, food cravings, hormonal changes, body aches, weight changes, and finally labor and delivery made her aware of the 24/7 responsibilities of parenting that were in store for us. Even after our children were born, it took time for me to understand that parenting is *our* responsibility, not just her responsibility.

Our experience isn't all that unique. A study of couples where both work 40 hours a week and each spend 15 hours a week doing housework found that after the baby arrived, moms do more and dads do less. Moms continued to do 15 hours a week and "added 22 hours a week of childcare." Most dads picked up only about 14 hours of childcare, but started doing less housework.[1]

Giving 100 Percent—Together

I (*Patrick*) can't say that I hadn't been warned about what marriage and parenting would require. I remember sitting in a Chicago park with my mentor while attending Moody Bible Institute. It was Sunday night, and we were meeting to talk about relationships. I don't recall most of what he said that night. However, one phrase has stuck with me: "Marriage is not 50/50. A Christian marriage is 100/100. You put in 100 percent and your wife puts in 100 percent. This is how Christ loved the church. He didn't just put in 50 percent."

Thanks a lot. This was not the positive, encouraging relationship talk I was looking for. But he was right. I have since discovered that it is physically impossible to remove a defiled onesie from a newborn and refill a sippy cup while dodging Nerf arrows without some assistance. As our family began to grow, it became obvious that one person could not realistically be expected to keep up on all of the housework, laundry, cooking, and child-rearing. As a guy, I needed the 100 percent reminder more than Ruth did. We can be a little slow to pick up on all of the "hints" for more help from our spouses.

While Patrick may have been slow to the game, that isn't the case anymore. Thankfully! I (*Ruth*) can't imagine what it

---

1. Brigid Schulte, "Once the baby comes, moms do more, dads do less around the house," *Washington Post* (May 7, 2015), www.washingtonpost.com/news/parenting/wp/2015/05/07/once-the-baby-comes-moms-do-more-dads-do-less-around-the-house/.

would be like if Patrick and I didn't parent together whole-heartedly. The role change from being a spouse to becoming a parent brings a huge change in responsibilities. Suddenly we are doing more dishes and more laundry. We are changing diapers, feeding children, and giving baths—lots of them. When our kids get older, we are juggling schedules, schoolwork, and extracurricular activities. We both need each other to give 100 percent just to make it through the tasks each day brings.

Even more important, our roles as parents aren't just about the work that needs to be done to live life. In order to fulfill our God-given mission as parents, it is our job to train our kids to be good citizens of earth and heaven, to nurture their God-given talents, and to train them in godliness. The Bible makes it very clear that both mom and dad are to be actively involved in teaching, shaping, and caring for their children. Consider the following passages of Scripture:

- Honor your father and your mother, so that you may live long in the land the LORD your God is giving you. (Exodus 20:12)
- My son, keep your father's command and do not forsake your mother's teaching. (Proverbs 6:20)
- Fathers, do not exasperate your children; instead, bring them up in the training and instruction of the Lord. (Ephesians 6:4)
- Fathers, do not embitter your children, or they will become discouraged. (Colossians 3:21)
- I am reminded of your sincere faith, which first lived in your grandmother Lois and in your mother Eunice and, I am persuaded, now lives in you also. (2 Timothy 1:5; see also 2 Timothy 3:15)

Each of these verses reminds us that it is not one parent who is nurturing and shepherding children. It is a team effort. The Bible doesn't prescribe every detail about who should do what when it comes to marriage or parenting. There is a lot of room for deciding the best way to live life as a married couple with a family. As a result, every spouse must give 100 percent to the other as they work together to determine how to best accomplish the demands of family life.

Managing the Daily Grind

Regardless of which stage of life a family is in, parents need clarity on daily responsibilities and expectations. For guys, I (*Patrick*) emphasize the words "clear" and "specific." This past summer, Ruth and I were in our front yard looking at our mulch beds. Ruth made the comment that they needed some cleaning up. The "outdoors" is sort of my domain—mowing, weeding, and landscaping are responsibilities that typically fall to me. We had just bought a few new plants and flowers, so she was anxious for me to get going on this outdoor project. A few days later, I decided to surprise Ruth while she was at the store.

I knew I didn't have much time, so as Ruth pulled out of the driveway, I quickly got to work. I took another look at our mulch beds, trying to remember exactly what needed to be "cleaned up." I vaguely remembered which plants needed some TLC and which needed to be pulled out. So I went for it. I dug out the dead butterfly bush and planted in its place a beautiful new hosta. Stepping back to admire my work, I noticed Ruth was just pulling into the driveway—home much sooner than I expected.

I watched her get out of the car. *Wait for it. Any minute, she is going to begin singing my praises.*

Still waiting for it.

Nothing.

Then I saw the look in her eyes. No love, just concern. Maybe even confusion. Then she said, "Honey, what are you doing?"

"Cleaning out the bed like you wanted," I answered.

"You dug up my butterfly bush!" she exclaimed.

I was already aware of that. What was news to me was that it wasn't dead. Oops!

I (*Ruth*) have had to learn the hard way that I must communicate *clearly* what I need Patrick to help me do. He always does plenty to help, but sometimes he doesn't do what is most pressing at the moment. I can't fault him for not knowing what I am thinking. If I know something needs to be done—Sophia needs a bath or Tyler needs help with his homework or the dogs need to go out—I need to tell him. I spent too many years sulking, feeling alone, and acting as if I'd been wronged, when what I really needed to do was to ask for specific help in a kind tone of voice.

How do we decide who should do what? How do we divide up the tasks? We begin by clearly identifying the needs and communicating how we can sacrificially work together to serve each other based on our strengths. The goal is not to create an environment where one spouse is saying, "Look at all I am doing!" The goal is to help each other carry the load.

I strongly dislike ironing! Fortunately Patrick is, shall we say, obsessed with living in a wrinkle-free world. He does a lot of ironing. When it comes to finances, Patrick is much better with the big picture. He can think through what we need to be saving for and engage in long-term planning. I am not good at that part of the finances, but it would be a disaster if he were paying the day-to-day bills, a chore I handle easily. So we work together, using our God-given strengths and gifts to serve our family.

Let's Talk about Sharing Responsibilities

Every couple needs to talk about better ways to share the enormous responsibilities of parenting together. Use the questions that follow as discussion points for charting a new course for your marriage.

- In what area of parenting do each of you most need your spouse's help right now?
- What would be most helpful for your spouse to start doing?
- What would be most helpful for your spouse to stop doing?

As it relates to household duties, where could each of you use your spouse's help most right now?

- What would you prefer your spouse to start doing?
- What would you prefer your spouse to stop doing?
- What difference would these changes make in your day-to-day life and outlook—and in your feelings toward your spouse?

As we identify the needs of parenting together, it's wise to avoid making "hard edges" where there really should be "soft edges." The goal is not to create a legalistic list of "you must always" and "you must nots." The goal is to follow the Bible's clear instruction to work together so we can be that well-synchronized team.

It's far too easy to become weary in parenting, and when a couple become weary in parenting, they also will become weary in marriage. In Galatians 6:9, the apostle Paul writes, "Let us not become weary in doing good, for at the proper time we will reap a harvest if we do not give up." No Christian wants to become weary and give up on God's plan for marriage and family. By parenting together we help to prevent either one of us from becoming discouraged, overwhelmed, or unnecessarily weary.

Envisioning the Same Goal

I (*Patrick*) was in fifth grade when my best friend and I found his dad's hunting bow in the garage. I had never shot a bow. Neither had he. It takes a tremendous amount of strength and skill. Unfortunately, we had neither. However, the "stuffed animals" hanging on the game room walls in my friend's house proved that his dad knew how to shoot a bow.

Like most boys our age, we were curious. After some discussion and a few failed attempts, we finally mustered enough strength to pull back the bow. We were so focused on pulling the string back that neither the direction nor the destination of the arrow were on our radar. The arrow must have shot at least forty feet into the air. It went nearly straight up, but leaned just enough to the southwest to land on the neighbor's roof. It was a moment mixed with great awe and great anxiety.

I've found that parenting is a lot like that experience. When we first started out as parents, we really didn't have a clue what we were doing. Our kids were adorable, advanced, near perfect, and the exception to everyone else's parenting problems. Or so we thought! In time we learned what every other parent already knew: no matter what we plan for, children are full of surprises. No wonder parenting is exhausting, sometimes dangerous, often humbling, and always an adventure. Like aiming in the right direction before shooting an arrow, we need to think about both direction and destination when it comes to raising our children.

It is essential that both parents envision the same goals for their family and children. If we don't have clarity of vision, or if we have competing visions, we will run into conflict. It may not happen immediately, but eventually conflict will arise.

Not only do we need to share the same vision, we also must have the right vision. There is no shortage of visions being suggested for children in today's culture. Consider how prevalent and all-consuming the following "visions" for children are in many families:

The Academic Overachiever—These parents have a vision for their son or daughter to get into the best of the best schools. A high priority is placed on excellence and hard work in the areas of education and extracurricular activities.

The Champion Athlete—These parents have a vision for their son or daughter to be a highly successful athlete.

Lots of time, energy, and money are invested in sports activities, including travel leagues and specialty camps and clinics.

The Cultured Socialite—These parents have a vision for their son or daughter to be well rounded and highly cultured. Kids are involved in everything from French lessons to piano and dance. The goal is lots of cultural exposure, travel, and other diverse experiences.

The Star Performer—These parents have a vision for their son or daughter to be famous in the arts—rock star, beauty pageants, actor, or actress. Time and energy are directed toward helping their child get "discovered."

The Perfect Christian—These parents have a vision for their son or daughter to be dedicated to ministry, so they are in church every time the doors are open. They stress volunteer work, Bible study, and homeschooling or Christian schools.

These visions, and others, are competing for our allegiance as a couple to put Jesus first in our family (even church work, when taken to extremes, can become an idol). We want our children to do well and succeed in life. We want them to become morally upright and emotionally, physically, relationally, and spiritually healthy adults. But we have to come together and honestly ask ourselves, "Whose standard will influence our family? Are we following Jesus and carefully stewarding the gifts of our family, or are we just blindly following someone else's standard of what we should be doing?"

While these are not necessarily bad visions to pursue, we want to be sure our vision for our children includes their overall personal and spiritual well-being. The "Academic Overachievers" might be challenged to develop a distinctly Christian worldview with which to critique what they are learning. They might need to be reminded that intelligence doesn't equal wisdom. "Champion Athletes" and "Star Performers" may need to think about how their faith affects their behavior on the field or on the stage—and off. "Cultured Socialites" might look for ways their Christian faith is expressed in the arts and ways they can share it with other cultures. They might need to be cautioned against elitism. Even "Perfect Christians" need to examine which ministries and ministry activities best suit the schedule, needs, abilities, and calling of family members. And all need to be reminded that they are saved by grace, not works.

Christ places far less value on who is smartest, most athletic, most culturally sophisticated, most talented, or even most "religious." Jesus delights in those who seek him and his righteousness first, knowing that "all these things" will then fall into place (Matthew 6:33). Jesus' righteousness includes service, humility, sacrificial love, and the hunger for what is right—qualities we can take into any arena of life. As parents, we need to be careful that we measure our child not against the world's standards but against God's. It takes both parents working together to fulfill the vision God has given us for marriage and family.

In our efforts to become united in parenting our children according to the vision God has given for the family, we have been encouraged by a book written by English writer and pastor J. C. Ryle. Published in 1888 and called *The Duties of Parents*, the book describes godly goals for raising children. Referring to Proverbs 22:6, Ryle, a father of five, wrote these words:

Train well for this life, and train well for the life to come; train well for earth, and train well for heaven; train them for God, train them for Christ, and train them for eternity.

One phrase, "train them for eternity," has stuck with us, reminding both of us to teach and train our children for what really matters. In a culture where the opportunities (most of which are good) are endless, it is easy, if not tempting, to lose sight of eternity. Parenting for what really matters isn't a job for one. We have to pull together to make sure we keep aiming for the most important target.

Just the *Two* of Us

We won't succeed as a well-synchronized team if we are aiming in different directions. Set aside some time for you and your spouse to talk about the following:

- Regardless of their occupation or what they accomplish, who do we want our children to be when they leave home?

- What do we see are the greatest challenges to our vision for parenting? What can we each do to support each other in fighting for God's best for our children?

Establish Priorities That Support Your Vision

With so many opportunities available to our children, most of which are very good, it's hard to know what is best. We really wrestled with whether to allow our oldest son and daughter to play in a travel soccer league during the summer. As a couple, we went back and forth, trying to figure out what would be best for our marriage and our family as a whole. We share the same vision, but we were concerned about different priorities. I (*Patrick*) was concerned about whether not playing now would hurt them in the future. Ruth was more concerned with cost, the overlap with our youngest son's baseball season, and the time away we had planned as a couple.

Unfortunately, there is no Bible verse with a black-and-white answer for decisions like this one. That is why both parents need to be involved in such decisions. We each need to be giving 100 percent as we seek God's wisdom to chart the best path (James 1:17).

We took time to pray about this opportunity and decision. We talked about it and consulted several couples who were in a similar situation. We even talked with our kids about the potential impact on their involvement in church and student ministry, and our time together as a family. In the end, we chose to skip travel soccer in the summer. We used what we felt was God's vision to discern what we should or shouldn't do in this situation.

Every couple with kids struggles with these types of decisions. No family can do it all. Engaging our kids in certain opportunities or activities means the exclusion of other opportunities and activities. That is why it is so important to come together and have the necessary conversations to clarify which priorities are most important to us as a couple and which are most important to our family. Then we can make decisions that will help us move in the direction of God's vision for our marriage and family.

Life will follow what we love. A love for sports, dance, or even church activities can squeeze out the time needed for a husband and wife to get away. When nights and weekends are booked solid, a couple has no time to date or just enjoy being together. An out-of-balance commitment to activities can leave a couple feeling exhausted and overwhelmed, with too little to give each other. Even good activities that support raising our kids in the right way have a direct impact on our marriage. We must make our choices carefully. The goal is to come together, love each other, and parent as a team.

Guard against Division in Discipline and Parenting

There is a reason I (*Patrick*) called my dad "Gentle Gene the Tender Machine." He was just that—gentle. My mom was a strict disciplinarian. Today I am thankful she kept me on the straight and narrow. But as a child, not so much! As a couple, my parents could not have been any more different when it came to parenting. Yet they often, not always, had a balancing effect on each other. A balance of tough and tender enabled them to parent together in a way that didn't cause division in their marriage.

Differences in the discipline of children is perhaps one of the most common causes of conflict for couples. It is not unusual for a husband and a wife to be very different in their discipline styles—one strict, the other more permissive. Some of us tend to parent in the same way our parents did. Others parent in the opposite way from how their parents did it. No matter which way we parent, the goal is to be in agreement with each other and in line with God's Word.

Differences in parenting became a glaring challenge for a couple I (*Patrick*) met with several years ago. They were a blended family trying to manage not only their marriage but also each other's kids. Divorce was not an option. At least that is what they would have said twelve years earlier. With several children and a previously failed marriage, the wife was not willing to even consider the thought of divorce. This marriage would not only be different, it would be better.

Then it happened. Not all at once, but over the course of weeks, months, and years. The conflicts, while small at first, escalated with time, growing into a question she had sworn she would never ask again: "Do I stay or do I leave?" What once had been unthinkable now seemed unavoidable.

The cause might surprise you. It wasn't financial friction that was tearing them apart. It wasn't the seduction of another lover. It wasn't her husband's work, their different interests, or conflicting communication. It was something far less likely—it was their kids.

For several years, this couple tried to ignore what was obvious—their parenting styles, philosophies, priorities, and even more significant, their differences in discipline were pulling them apart. He was frustrated that she seemed to show favoritism to her children. She was growing resentful that he was not enforcing consequences for their children when they failed to do what was asked. She thought the kids needed more responsibilities and boundaries. He thought she was being too strict.

This conflict over differences in parenting isn't true for every couple, but for many it can be a huge source of marital strife. In worst-case scenarios, these parenting differences lead to separation.

Protect the Authority of Your Parenting

In God's plan for a family, biblical discipline (correction, training, and instruction) is to be lived out within loving relationships. God has given parents authority in our families. He has placed us as a couple to reflect his character to our children. We have a tremendous responsibility and privilege to lead our family in the ways of the Lord. But it isn't easy. Charles Spurgeon was right when he wrote, "If we never have headaches through rebuking [disciplining] our little children, we shall have plenty of heartaches when they grow up."[2]

One of the dangers of permissive parenting is displacing our parental authority to our children. The children's behavior, attitudes, preferences, and desires become the driving force in the family. In this kind of environment, it's not what the parent says, it's about what the child wants. We all know that this is a recipe for disaster as kids grow up. Just as devastating is what can happen between a husband and a wife in this environment.

When a couple begins to transfer their parental authority to their kids, their life and relationship begins to revolve

---

2. Charles H. Spurgeon, *John Ploughman's Talks: Everyday Advice Based on Biblical Truth* (New Kensington, PA: Whitaker House, 2012), 28.

around what their children want and desire. The parents slip back into having a child-centered marriage. A husband who had come to me for advice said he felt as if his wife was always putting the needs of their oldest son in front of his. The son was attending a local community college, but often asked for financial assistance—help with rent, phone bill, an occasional car payment. The wife would sacrifice time, energy, and money for what their son wanted. The husband had a different idea on how to handle the situation. They were not unified in how to parent their son, and over time, this situation put tremendous strain on their marriage.

Regardless of our children's ages, we need to remember that we are the parents. We must guard against transferring our authority to our kids—letting their every desire, preference, and wish chart the course. Part of protecting our marriage while parenting is to be consistent with expectations and consequences.

Kids figure out too quickly who is strict and who is soft. After a no from Ruth about going to a movie, one of our kids texted me for another try. While I was inclined to say yes, I had enough sense to check with Ruth first.

Ruth and I have learned that we can be very different in our responses to our children's desires and behaviors. We've found that it is always better to talk as a couple before granting permission for certain activities or deciding on what consequences are necessary. This gives us an opportunity to cool down when necessary, discuss what is appropriate, and be united in our response to our child. This better enables us to maintain our parental authority as a team. We are working together to protect our marriage from division. We are working together to shape and build our kids to develop Christlike character.

Parenting is just too big and too messy to do alone. Kids will expose our weaknesses—revealing how selfish and sinful we still really are! In the midst of all the joy and goodness, they will humble us, test us, and at times divide us. While we don't always do parenting perfectly, working together as parents helps us to live out the missing vow to love each other with kids in the house. If we are going to live out God's good but messy mission, we have to keep in step with each other like a well-synchronized team—covering, complementing, strengthening, and encouraging each other along the way.

— 6 —

GRACE FOR THOSE NOT-SO-PERFECT MOMENTS

It is impossible to love deeply without sacrifice.
Elisabeth Elliot, *Marriage:*
A Revolution and a Revelation

During World War II, on December 20, 1943, two enemy pilots met in the air over Oldenburg, Germany. The American pilot was Charles "Charlie" Brown. The German pilot was Franz Stigler. Both men were experienced and well-respected pilots. Brown, the American, was flying a B-17 Flying Fortress, and Franz, the German, was flying a Messerschmitt Bf 109 G-6 fighter. The problem was, they were on opposing sides of a world conflict. The nations they represented were at war.

Brown and his crew had been sent on a bombing mission

that would take them into the heart of enemy territory. Not long after entering German air space, the American bomber came under heavy attack. The damage done sent the B-17 into a nosedive that took the plane from over twenty thousand feet to within a mile above German homes, trees, and citizens.

Somehow Brown managed to keep the bomber from crashing even though it was badly damaged, what could be described as "chewed to pieces." It was missing a stabilizer, had an exposed front nose, was bleeding hydraulics, and had huge holes through the fuselage. It was unlikely the B-17 would ever make it out of Germany, let alone survive the flight back over the sea to safety in England.

It wasn't long before the crippled American bomber was spotted by the German pilot, Franz Stigler. Barely keeping his plane in the air, Brown was exposed and vulnerable. This had the makings of a disastrous ending.

The skilled German pilot put his finger on the trigger and locked the American plane in his gun sight. With his finger on the trigger, it would take only a moment to win this fight. Adam Makos, the author who tells this true story in the book *A Higher Call*, describes the scene:

Franz squinted and aimed through his gun sight. He lowered his finger onto the trigger, a pound of pressure away from igniting the guns.[1]

But then something unusual happened. Franz Stigler, an enemy of the American plane, took his finger off the trigger!

---

1. Adam Makos with Larry Alexander, *A Higher Call: An Incredible True Story of Combat and Chivalry in the War-Torn Skies of World War II* (New York: Berkley, 2012), 200.

Instead of destroying the enemy bomber, he decided to protect it. Makos continues:

> Floating behind the B-17, Franz looked at the bomber with the curiosity of his boyhood, a time when he would run from his house at the sound of an airplane. In a rush of long-dormant emotions, Franz forgot he was a German fighter pilot.[2]

After sparing the life of his enemy, Franz Stigler realized the crippled American plane would face a wall of enemy fire defending the "Atlantic Wall." He then flew side by side with his enemy to protect the B-17 from being shot down. If his fellow German fighters on the ground chose to shoot down the American plane, they would also have to shoot him down. It was a daring, brave, and highly unusual decision during wartime:

> Side by side the 109 and the B-17 soared over the soldiers defending the Atlantic Wall, then over the beach obstacles and the crashing surf. The sight was a beautiful one, the little fighter protecting the big bomber. They flew together out over the gray sea as if they were leaving one world for another.[3]

Somehow, by God's grace, the bomber made it home. The pilot and crew lived because an enemy pilot decided to spare them by taking his finger off the trigger. The two pilots, who

---

2. Ibid., 201.
3. Ibid., 205.

met first as enemies, met again forty years later—this time as friends.

I (*Patrick*) love the courage, compassion, and grace demonstrated in this story by one pilot protecting the life of another. I can't help but wonder how differently this story would have ended if Franz Stigler had pulled the trigger. Think of how different their lives and the lives of their kids, grandkids, and great-grandkids would have been had Stigler made a different decision.

In the middle of a tense battle, only "one pound of pressure" stood between two very different endings—life or death. I sometimes wonder how different our marriages would be if, in the heat of battle, we learned to exercise grace by taking our finger off the trigger. What if we saw our spouse not as an enemy, but as an ally? What if we chose to extend our love, protection, and strength when our spouse is weak and vulnerable?

Bringing Life by Bringing Grace

The change from marriage to marriage with kids in the house brings added responsibility and pressure to every part of life. Having kids in the house creates unexpected stress, tension, and conflict. When we're exhausted and running on fumes, we tend to feel as if life is out of control. We feel tense, vulnerable, and more on edge. This can make us more volatile. With kids in the mix, our fuse can be short—really short. It may not take much for us to "pull the trigger" on each other.

While on vacation in northern Michigan, we became

firsthand witnesses to a showdown. We were shopping and noticed a three-year-old girl standing at the door of a store. Her glasses were a bit cockeyed and her hair was wild from the wind. She was looking longingly into the store. Her mom was just inside, shopping, presumably attempting to enjoy doing so with some peace and quiet. Then the three-year-old broke her silence:

"Moooooom, can I give you a hug yet? Mom, I want to give you a hug! Mom, can I come in and give you a hug now? Mooooom?"

Finally, unable to control herself, she burst into the store and ran to her mom. Wrapping herself around her mom's leg, she squeezed tight. Mission accomplished!

Then Dad enters the story. Placing one hand on her daughter's back, the mother raised her other hand and pointed to her husband to get his attention. Our eyes followed her finger. He was sitting on a bench just outside the door minding his own business, which was the problem.

Trying to mouth her frustration but unable to contain her emotion, the mother finally yelled, "Alan! Alan! Can't you watch the kids for just five minutes? Come get her!"

Alan was busted. He had been looking at his phone, unaware that his daughter had rushed into the store. Feeling the heat of embarrassment of being publicly shamed by his wife, he threw his hands up. Then he attempted to throw his daughter under the bus.

"What are you doing? Get over here and sit down!" he yelled. "You need to sit right here next to me while Mommy is trying to shop."

The look from his wife made it clear she was not buying

it. Not only was the three-year-old in trouble, so was he! The story ended with an angry husband, an irritated wife, and a sobbing child. It's probably not exactly what they envisioned when they set out for a day of shopping and walking along the beach.

We both had to laugh. The scene was not just funny, it was all too familiar. We couldn't help but see ourselves in that moment. Stressed. Tired. Irritable. Just wanting a little time alone. Then something small and innocent sends us over the edge.

Kids have a way of applying just enough pressure to send us headlong into conflict with each other. We don't even want to imagine what the rest of that family's afternoon was like. Moments like these, when we find ourselves stretched, stressed, and ready to attack give us an opportunity to bring life to each other by bringing grace to each other—by living out the missing vow.

Grace means taking our finger off the trigger. Grace brings protection rather than punishment. Grace offers patience and relief from taking everything too seriously. Grace allows us to stop to breathe and to learn to laugh. Grace doesn't make assumptions. Grace extends understanding and offers forgiveness.

If you are like us, learning to walk in grace is toughest when we have kids in the house. But this is also one of the most important seasons in life to extend grace toward each other. Every relationship needs grace—lots of it. Without grace, no relationship would ever make it.

Grace Can't Stand Alone

Grace is a gift God extends to us so that we can be in relationship with him. When it comes to our relationship with God, we are the needy ones. We are vulnerable and exposed. We are sinners unable to remedy our situation on our own. So by grace God moves toward us. He takes the first step. God, in Jesus, forgives us of our sins. His grace brings us life when we need it most. Through faith, we can receive this unmerited move of God's love toward us.

> For it is by grace you have been saved, through faith—
> and this is not from yourselves, it is the gift of God—not
> by works, so that no one can boast. (Ephesians 2:8–9)

Biblical grace is useless in isolation. Grace needs more than one person to "work." It is necessary and valuable only in the context of relationships. Without the presence of another sinful person to act upon and relate to, grace is of no use. One writer describes it this way:

> Grace is the dimension of divine activity that enables
> God to confront human indifference and rebellion with
> an inexhaustible capacity to forgive and to bless. God is
> gracious in action.[4]

Grace is not just what God is; it is the action God does. Grace is not just a static attribute of God's nature; it is how God acts in relation to his creation. The saving activity of God

---

4. W. A. Elwell and B. J. Beitzel, *Baker Encyclopedia of the Bible* (Grand Rapids: Baker, 1988), 898.

through Jesus on the cross accomplishes for us what we could never do for ourselves. God's grace meets us in our need. It blesses. It forgives. It literally saves us, making relationship possible and beautiful.

God's grace and forgiveness enable us to stay in relationship with a holy and perfect God. Without grace in action, no relationship can maintain its existence. A marriage without grace would too easily nosedive into conflict, bitterness, resentment, and isolation. Where there is no grace, no mercy, no patience, no forgiveness, there cannot be an enduring and vibrant relationship.

If we are to be like Christ in marriage, we must move toward each other in grace. Grace brings life into our relationship and helps to sustain a marriage through its difficult seasons. Grace enables us to live out the missing vow to keep our love alive with kids in the house. Grace enables us to recognize each other's needs and to respond with love—a love that relieves and revives.

Grace Makes Room for Faults

Years ago, when Ruth and I were first married, we agreed that I would do the hard work of landscaping (digging beds, planting, and mulching). Ruth would do the tedious work of watering, weeding, and pruning. In hindsight, I had made a terrible agreement! With multiple family moves, landscaping the house was becoming more laborious. With kids, a perfect mulch bed was unrealistic. I grew tired of digging beds and planting bushes only to see my work ruined by baseballs, footprints, and squashed ferns. I became apathetic about the things that were growing around the house.

You can imagine my dismay when, while shopping at Costco, Ruth (with the excitement of her high school cheerleading days) blurts outs, "Honey, look! They have Knock Out rose bushes! We're missing one in the front. And look at the price!"

I must admit, I had no idea what she was talking about. A rose bush missing? But it was clear we were going to buy a new rose bush. This meant I would be planting a new rose bush. Sold!

Before unloading frozen fruit, toilet paper, and water bottles, we escorted our new rose bush to its desired place in the mulch bed. We placed it perfectly in relation to the other plants, where its new roots would grow deep and strong. That is, of course, assuming I remembered to plant the rose bush.

Now I (*Ruth*) was doing my best not to nag Patrick about planting the bush. I would occasionally mention that the rose bush needed to be planted, but I really didn't say much about it. After all, I figured it was hard to miss, sitting smack dab in the middle of our raised mulch bed in the front of the house. It was large and full of bright pink roses. It was a beauty! Whether Patrick completely forgot or was avoiding the task, I have no idea. Either way, the poor bush slowly died in the hot summer sun.

One particularly hot summer day, weeks after our purchase, I was watering the bushes next to my dead, not-so-Knock-Out-anymore rose bush. Out of the corner of my eye I spotted what I thought for sure was a tiny bud. Although the entire bush was brown, with barely a leaf on it, that dead rose bush was alive! It was hanging on by a thread, just waiting for me to rescue it! I rushed into the backyard to tell Patrick.

Judging from Ruth's excitement, I (*Patrick*) thought maybe we won the lottery (even though we don't play)! My enthusiasm over the news was less about the rose bush still being alive than it was about the opportunity to redeem myself. And I did. I immediately dropped what I was doing and planted the bush. Would you believe it? That bush came back to life! Today it is still flourishing with all the beauty that first drew Ruth to it.

Often, when watering our rose bush, I am reminded of how even small things can come between a couple. Marriage is full of failures. Some failures are big, but most are small. Something as small and insignificant as a rose bush can be a source of conflict in a marriage without grace.

A graceless marriage doesn't make room for mistakes. It is a crowded space, where there is little room to breathe. Where there is no place for error, the relationship suffocates. But grace paints an entirely different picture:

> Always be humble and gentle. Be patient with each other, making allowance for each other's faults because of your love. (Ephesians 4:2 NLT)

At the root of most relational stress and conflict is sin, particularly the sin of pride. "Pride," as John Stott wisely notes, "is more than the first of seven deadly sins: it is itself the essence of all sin."[5] Pride tempts us to see life only through our lens, which leads us to slip back into a me-centered marriage.

Humility, in contrast, is other-centered, not me-centered. In a relationship, humility allows us to be aware of our own

---

5. John Stott, "Pride, Humility, and God," *Sovereign Grace Magazine* (September/October 2000), http://www.cslewisinstitute.org/webfm_send/375.

faults and make allowances for the faults of others. Humble, gentle, gracious love tolerates shortcomings, creates space for mistakes, endures failures, and seeks to maintain relationship. Humble love allows us to elevate our spouse's need for care and concern above our own, especially during the challenging season of marriage with kids.

Humility is also quick to listen and slow to speak. James 1:19 commands us to be "quick to listen, slow to speak and slow to become angry." If we fail to be humble, we will not hear or understand where our spouse is coming from or where the real source of conflict or concern lies.

Three Types of Listening

When it comes to loving each other, listening to each other is essential. We cannot extend grace and bring life to our spouse if we don't truly hear our spouse's needs and concerns. We can hear the needs of our spouse more clearly if we are humble, free from distractions, and inquisitive.

Be a humble listener. Pride not only makes us blind, it can make us deaf too. Humility listens long before speaking. It enables us to hear and understand where our spouse is coming from. When we listen humbly, we are putting our spouse, not ourselves, at the center of a conversation.

Be an undistracted listener. While the ability to multitask is often impressive, when it comes to listening to your spouse, multitasking should be avoided. Life with kids in the house is busy and full of distractions. Listening well requires us to stop or slow down. Turn off the email. Put away the phone. Shut down the computer. Wait until the kids are in bed so that your spouse can be the focus of your undivided attention.

Be an inquisitive listener. An inquisitive listener is someone who not only comprehends what is being said but cares about what is being said. This doesn't mean you love everything your spouse loves. It is unlikely for a wife to love football the way her husband does or for a husband to love Pinterest the way his wife does. It does mean you value what is important to your spouse and actively engage in listening to your spouse. Asking questions as you listen is a great way to show your interest in what your spouse values.

Grace Guards against Making Small Stuff Big Stuff

Out of sheer desperation, I (*Ruth*) recently held a "family summit" to discuss the habit of leaving dirty dishes in the sink instead of putting them in the dishwasher. I consider it an easy task to rinse your dish and place it in the dishwasher where it belongs. Unfortunately, this doesn't seem to work well in our house. I am usually the only one in the house who follows the rule.

After much frustration, I was feeling irritated by the whole thing. I decided I needed to lay down the law! My approach wasn't harsh. It was more like a pleading for all parties to please, please, pleeease put your dishes in the dishwasher after you get a drink, snack, or eat a meal. I felt my case was strong. When the situation improved for about two whole days and then returned to its original state, I was just plain old mad!

To put things into perspective, I had to remind myself that this was not a huge deal. The path of grace would be to gently remind my children and my husband (ahem) to put their dishes in the dishwasher without making it seem as if they were committing a grave and serious sin if they forgot. My preference on dirty dishes is important, but it's not *that* important.

Maybe it's not the dishes for you. It could be a host of other little things—the squashed toothpaste tube, the empty toilet paper roll, scattered piles of dirty laundry, a personality difference. Overlooking the small offenses that we encounter in daily life (as well as seeking not to cause offense) is about learning to see one another through the lens of the gospel. It is about treating each other with kindness, gentleness, and grace. It is choosing to move toward one another rather than selfishly pushing one another away.

When I (*Patrick*) work with couples in premarital counseling, I always encourage them to remember that there is a big difference between breaking each other's rules and breaking God's rules. One is about preference, the other is about sin. Learning to distinguish between the two can help us to overlook some of the less serious sources of conflict. It also allows space for growth. Learning to compromise and grow toward your spouse can be accomplished only in a grace-filled environment.

We all blow it in marriage. None of us has a perfect

record. We are going to fail at being the perfect husband, the perfect wife, and the perfect parent. Our spouse will not always do what we want. Personality differences will be glaring. Preferences will be annoying. Offenses will be inevitable. Sin will happen.

Grace does not demand perfection in someone else, but makes space for progress. Not only are our kids growing up, we are growing up too. So we need to build into our marriage the space to grow and mature. We are not suggesting that sin should be ignored, but we must learn to overlook some offenses. If we don't, life will be unbearable!

We don't have to fire at every occurrence of failure. Proverbs 19:11 reminds us that there is wisdom in creating room to breathe in relationships: "A person's wisdom yields patience; it is to one's glory to overlook an offense." We bring life to our relationships when we take our finger off the trigger.

God's power and presence in us enable us to act with wisdom and patience and exercise self-control. By grace, we don't have to "get even" for every offense. Instead, there is a patient love that allows us to overlook minor disagreements or annoyances. As Ken Sande notes, grace, in overlooking an offense, means "to deliberately decide not to talk about it, dwell on it, or let it grow into pent-up bitterness."[6]

As a couple, we rest in the grace and perfection of Jesus. Because Jesus has loved us with patience, mercy, and humility, we can do the same for our spouse (Philippians 2:5). Walking in grace is not about putting up with our spouse's weakness as much as it is trusting that God's Spirit is at work in our spouse to do his will, in his time, in his way (John 16:7–9).

---

6. Ken Sande, *The Peace Maker: The Biblical Guide to Resolving Personal Conflict* (Grand Rapids: Baker, 2004), 83.

Just the *Two* of Us

Every wife, every husband needs the protection of grace in their marriage. Take some time to talk about ways you can extend grace to each other.

- What are some practical ways you can make room for each other's flaws and failures?
- When have you especially appreciated your spouse's grace, protection, or forgiveness?
- What specific things could the two of you begin doing to bring more grace and life into your relationship?

The Hardest Words to Say— "Please Forgive Me"

I (*Patrick*) had called home when I left the office to let Ruth know I would be stopping by the house in a few minutes. I could barely hear Ruth's voice on the phone. "What is going on?" I asked.

My curious (and concerned) ears heard enough to know there was trouble on the home front. As it turned out, our five-year-old daughter had snatched our oldest son's lemonade out of the fridge—without permission. What followed was a whole lot of relational mess that was going to take time to sort out and mop up. A simple "I'm sorry, please forgive me" would have saved everyone a lot of time and energy!

Kids aren't the only ones who struggle to keep the peace.

Romans 12:18 reminds us of the struggle we face: "If it is possible, as far as it depends on you, live at peace with everyone."

Most adults, including us, are less than stellar at living in peace. We seem to have the hardest time saying the simple words, "Forgive me." Many of us would rather defend our sin than deal with our sin. And asking and granting forgiveness to those we love most is often the most difficult.

Yet walking in grace requires us to learn to give and receive forgiveness. Perhaps one of the greatest examples of the blessing of forgiveness and the poison of unforgiveness is found in Matthew 18:21–35.

Peter, one of Jesus' disciples, asks, "Lord, how many times shall I forgive my brother . . . who sins against me? Up to seven times?" Peter's question assumes that there must be a limit to God's grace. He's essentially asking, "How do I know when I have forgiven enough?" Jesus responds by telling a parable:

> The kingdom of heaven is like a king who wanted to settle accounts with his servants. As he began the settlement, a man who owed him ten thousand bags of gold was brought to him. Since he was not able to pay, the master ordered that he and his wife and his children and all that he had be sold to repay the debt.
>
> At this the servant fell on his knees before him. "Be patient with me," he begged, "and I will pay back everything." The servant's master took pity on him, canceled the debt and let him go.

Forgiveness, like grace, is about restoring a broken, imbalanced, and indebted relationship. Forgiveness is not forgetting about sin. It's not losing the memory of a bad choice, hurtful words, or difficult experience. Forgiveness is refusing to punish the person who sinned against us.

Forgiveness is costly. In Jesus' parable, the master absorbs the debt and releases the servant. In marriage, forgiveness is about releasing our spouse instead of getting even. It is not easy to say to our spouse, "You are free. I am deleting your bad credit. You are released." It may seem far easier to make our spouse pay.

Walking in grace by offering forgiveness is costly, but harboring unforgiveness is even more costly. What is shocking about the rest of Jesus' parable is that the man who was released from his debt runs into a man who owes him money. Instead of extending the same grace and forgiveness, he chokes the man and demands to be paid back. The man can't pay, so he has the poor guy thrown in prison until he can pay back the debt. The parable ends with strong words for those who follow in this servant's foolish footsteps. The point is clear: how could we not forgive, considering how much we have been forgiven?

Follow Jesus' Example of Grace

In Jesus, God dressed himself in humility to reconcile and restore a lost and broken relationship. The joy and intimacy we can now enjoy in our relationship with God is the result of God moving toward us. He "humbled himself by becoming obedient to death—even death on a cross" (Philippians 2:8). He died to himself that we might experience life.

We need grace. Marriage with kids in the house can be chaotic, stressful, and overwhelming. The good and messy mission of living out a God-honoring marriage and family is no simple task. We need God's grace to do the job well. And we need to extend the grace of undeserved love toward each other in order to fulfill our vows to love each other for better or for kids.

In the heat of the moment, "one pound of pressure" is sometimes all that separates us from chaos. When we choose grace, we choose to keep loving, serving, blessing, and giving. We are choosing to bring life to each other when we both need it the most.

— 7 —

TIME, REST, AND RHYTHM

Making Our Days Count

One life on this earth is all that we get . . . we are fools if we do not live it as fully and bravely and beautifully as we can.

Frederick Buechner, *The Hungering Dark*

We needed to get away—recharge the batteries, catch our breath, and refocus. We were looking for a little balance, if such a thing existed. We had taken several modest vacations as a couple, but things had changed. We were now a couple with children. So we decided to drive to Colorado for a family vacation.

Looking back, yoga might have been a better option. Most Sundays, just getting our whole family to church on time was a challenge. As a growing family with a diminishing budget, there was no way we could afford to fly anywhere—not with three kids. And we simply could not pass up the opportunity a generous couple in our church had given us to spend a week at their condo in the beautiful ski town of Lake Dillon, Colorado. So we did what other less brave families cautioned us not to do: we loaded up the minivan and hit the road for a cross-country trek to the Colorado mountains.

Doing the math, we calculated it would take us roughly twenty hours to drive to Colorado from our home in Ohio. In a car without iPads, DVD players, or a working stereo, we needed entertainment—lots of it. So before departure, we handed each child his or her very own "play kit," a plastic container filled with coloring books, word games, puzzles, and books. In theory, these would keep our kids well occupied until at least Denver, which would provide the two of us with hours of meaningful discussion and peaceful driving. In reality, our plan worked for about an hour. A "play kit" doesn't really work for a six-month-old.

An indoor pool in Omaha saved us. We dangled this carrot in front of our two- and four-year-olds for close to six hundred miles. "Who wants to swim tonight?" we asked every fifteen minutes. "It's going to be soooo much fun!"

Our tactics worked. We drove about halfway without any major meltdowns—from the kids or from us. We were ten hours down with ten to go.

On day two we were hopeful, and for more than nine hours we had every right to be. It was smooth sailing. The kids were nearly perfect, just as we expected they would be before we brought them into the world. With one more hour to go, we were excited that our destination was actually within reach. We were ready to get there.

We took a short break for dinner and got right back on the road. Shortly after we resumed our travel, just as it was beginning to get dark, we felt the van struggling on a steep climb, almost losing power. We were in heavy traffic, climbing quickly into the mountains. We live where roads are flat—really flat. The cars surrounding us were clearly more adept at driving quickly up and down mountains and around curves than we were.

Then it happened again. The van was struggling, and this time we lost power completely. Ruth was praying feverishly by this time and pretty much crying out for mercy. The kids were crying out of fear. And I was stone silent. Faking courage and confidence, I steered the car as far off the road as I could without rolling us down the side of the mountain.

This was not the relaxed, restful vision we had imagined (and needed) for our vacation. If we hadn't been nineteen hours from home, we likely would have turned around and gone back. But the van was not going anywhere, so we didn't either. For nearly an hour we waited for the tow truck. Every episode of *America's Most Wanted* flashed through my mind as we sat quietly huddled on the side of a dark mountain.

Finally the tow truck arrived. The driver reminded me of Cooter Davenport from *The Dukes of Hazzard*. He was a little rough around the edges, but I was so happy to see him I almost hugged him. After a fast and frightening ride in the backseat of the tow truck straight down what seemed like the steepest mountain in Colorado, we arrived at our destination.

I'm not sure what people thought when we rolled into town—our van on the flatbed and the five of us in the back of the tow truck. I'm sure we looked a little wild-eyed. But we made it! We really did. We finally had gotten away for a vacation—a family vacation.

Time Is Ticking

The good and messy calling of marriage with kids often happens at lightning speed. Living in balance and finding time for rest (even on vacation) when kids come along is not easy! Life feels a bit like a wild van ride through the Rockies—far from restful or rhythmic. Sometimes we find ourselves just praying it will be over soon, and we live to tell about it! Even the language of *time, rest,* and *rhythm* may seem foreign to a couple with kids in the house.

The time kids need and deserve pulls a couple in many different directions. Every part of parenting stretches us and costs time. And the time demands are usually for important, good stuff:

> breast-feeding
> changing diapers
> doctor and dentist appointments
> soccer practice
> homework
> discipline
> school activities
> youth group
> even vacations

Our lives begin to revolve around our kids, leaving less and less time with and for each other. It's not uncommon for a couple to see their precious time together evaporate. We have less time to date, less time to talk, less time to be alone, less time to get away.

For us, the scarcity of time can even make buying an anniversary card a challenge. All summer we had been running and running and running. We'd been so busy planning for the upcoming school year, registering our kids for soccer camp, shopping for school supplies, trying to organize ministry details, and packing for vacation that we ran out of time for each other. Our anniversary was upon us before we even knew it.

When Ruth said, "I didn't get you an anniversary card," it was more of a confession than a statement. For a moment, I thought I heard angelic choirs singing the "Hallelujah Chorus." I entertained the thought of pretending that I hadn't forgotten, but I had to be honest.

"I didn't get you one either," I admitted. That is the moment we started talking about what we were going to do for our wedding anniversary, which happened to be the very next day. Not exactly romantic. Our busyness had us living out of sync. With little rest and almost no rhythm, our busyness was taking its toll on us.

The season of life we are in with kids in the house is a lot more hectic than the early days of marriage. We can remember when we went shopping when we wanted to. On a minute's notice, we went out for dinner or went on a run. We stayed up late watching television and slept in on weekends. No one awakened us by crying in the middle of the night or by pulling us out of bed at six on a Saturday morning. The luxury of time we used to enjoy together is hard to imagine now.

The time it takes to be a good parent can squeeze out the time it takes to be a good spouse. Endless activities and demanding schedules, like intruders, rob a couple of intimacy. Self-neglect and sacrifice become a way of life for most couples with kids. But living rushed, reactive, overstretched, and out-of-sync lives will eventually take its toll on a marriage.

Believe it or not, there is another option. God wants something more for us and has something more for us. It's not always easy, and it certainly doesn't happen by accident, but the hurried, busy, out-of-balance, hold-on-tight, I-am-losing-my-mind kind of life doesn't have to be our life (at least not all of the time). When we have kids in the house, we need to learn to view and steward our time differently. We need to create new boundaries to keep the busyness of life in balance and to keep our love alive!

Time Is Sacred

The tension between work and rest, busy and balanced is nothing new. It seems that we are not born with great wisdom when it comes to time. We don't naturally steward it well. It seems that sin distorts our view and use of time as it distorts our view of every other part of life. Given that time is so precious, especially when it feels as if it is flying by, it's not surprising that the Bible has a lot to say about time. We need help to view time as God sees it so that we can restore it to serve his purpose and put it to proper use in our marriage and family life.

The psalmist helps us to see God's view when he writes, "Teach us to number our days, that we may gain a heart of wisdom" (Psalm 90:12). In Hebrew, the word *wisdom* means "skilled." So to steward time wisely is to be skilled in how we use it. We begin faithful stewardship of our time when we make our days count. To waste or mismanage our days is to act foolishly and unskillfully.

In the New Testament, the apostle Paul warns:

> Be very careful, then, how you live—not as unwise but as wise, making the most of every opportunity, because the days are evil. Therefore do not be foolish, but understand what the Lord's will is. (Ephesians 5:15–17)

"Be very careful, then, how you live," Paul says. We need to pay attention to what we are, or aren't, doing with our time. We are to be productive not just for ourselves but for God's purposes, as we make the "most of every opportunity" that God has graciously given to us as a couple and as a family. We certainly don't want to be busy doing what is foolish in God's eyes.

Time is never entirely ours. God has numbered our days so that we might accomplish his will, not just what we want to do. Time is sacred. We are to use our time carefully and skillfully in order to build a God-honoring marriage, pass on faith to our kids, and impact the communities around us for God's glory.

Rest Is Holy

Did you know that the first place the word *holy* is mentioned in the Bible is in relation to time? In the creation account found in Genesis 2:2–3, *holy* is used to describe a day God designated for rest:

By the seventh day God had finished the work he had been doing; so on the seventh day he rested from all his work. Then God blessed the seventh day and made it holy, because on it he rested from all the work of creating that he had done.

In creation, God set apart time to be *holy*. Holiness in this sense isn't about moral purity; it is about setting apart. God made a provision in the midst of all of the busyness for rest. He established a rhythm to life by giving us a day set apart for rest. He wanted us to experience not just the whirlwind of time but the pattern of rest and rhythm.

Work, work, work, work, work, work—rest.

Go, go, go, go, go, go—stop.

Can you feel the cadence? Do you see the protection God has worked into creation? We can't race in a whirlwind all the time. We need time away to regroup and recover. It's not God who needs rest; the rhythm is not for him, it's for us.

Much to my parents' dismay, I (*Patrick*) loved rap music when I was young. When I was in elementary school, my mom found a Beastie Boys cassette tape I had bought and hid in a box in my closet. They weren't exactly a Christian band, so after some penance, I decided to stick with DC Talk and D-Boy.

My early interest in rap music hasn't helped my preaching much, but I did discover a great description of rhythm. Rhythm is what "makes lyrics sound musical and interesting. It's also what makes the lyrics a rap, rather than just words spoken in a random way over a beat."[1] Without rhythm, we are left with noise, not music. One is pleasing to the ear, the

---

1. Paul Edwards, *How to Rap: The Art and Science of the Hip-Hop MC* (Chicago: Review Press, 2009), 111.

other is painful. Like music, our life needs rhythm if it is to be lived well for God and for each other.

The pattern of work and rest found in creation is called "Sabbath." In the creation account we learn that God not only instituted a rhythm to life, he invited us to participate in that rhythm. If we want to keep the craziness of life from invading our intimacy as a couple, we need rest. We need a period of time to renew, refresh, reflect, and refocus. God has set forth a rhythm to life that includes Sabbath rest. This rhythm was instituted to help us, to keep us centered, balanced, and whole.

Throughout Israel's history, God continually reminded Israel of not only their responsibility to keep the Sabbath but also the reward of doing so. Creating space, slowing down, and building boundaries to provide rest in the midst of life was to be a blessing.

Remember the Sabbath day by keeping it holy. Six days you shall labor and do all your work, but the seventh day is a sabbath to the LORD your God. On it you shall not do any work, neither you, nor your son or daughter, nor your male or female servant, nor your animals, nor any foreigner residing in your towns. For in six days the LORD made the heavens and the earth, the sea, and all that is in them, but he rested on the seventh day. Therefore the LORD blessed the Sabbath day and made it holy. (Exodus 20:8–11)

Rest Is Freedom

Do you ever feel enslaved to an overcommitted schedule? Does it seem as if there just isn't enough time to do all that you need to do? Not enough time with the kids? Not enough time away from the kids? If you answered yes, you are not alone. Left unchecked, our schedule can be a brutal taskmaster.

In Exodus, God connects the Sabbath rest to creation. The perspective is a little different in Deuteronomy 5:15, where the Sabbath is connected to slavery:

> Remember that you were slaves in Egypt and that the LORD your God brought you out of there with a mighty hand and an outstretched arm. Therefore the LORD your God has commanded you to observe the Sabbath day.

In his book *The Rest of God*, Mark Buchanan makes this observation about rest and slavery in Israel's history:

> To refuse Sabbath is in effect to spurn the gift of freedom. It is to resume willingly what we once cried out for God to deliver us from. It is choosing what we once shunned. Slaves don't rest. Slaves can't rest. Slaves, by definition, have no freedom to rest. Rest, it turns out, is a condition of liberty. . . . Sabbath is a refusal to go back to Egypt.[2]

This Sabbath connection in Deuteronomy reminds us of the freedom available in rest, the freedom of balance, the

---

2. Mark Buchanan, *The Rest of God: Restoring Your Soul by Restoring Sabbath* (Nashville: Thomas Nelson, 2006), 90.

freedom we gain when we set up boundaries, and the blessing we receive when we guard the sacredness of time. Working hard and being busy doesn't have to mean slavery. There is a way to build into our lives boundaries that free us from the demanding, unproductive grind "Egypt" requires of us.

Throughout the Bible, this rhythm to life was meant to be a blessing. In Mark 2, Jesus gives us a clue on how this principle of rest and rhythm can still be applied today. One Sabbath, Jesus and his disciples were walking through a grainfield, and his disciples began to pick some heads of grain. Seeing this, the Pharisees accuse Jesus' disciples of breaking the Sabbath because they were picking grain. The whole exchange is recorded in Mark 2:23–28:

> One Sabbath Jesus was going through the grainfields, and as his disciples walked along, they began to pick some heads of grain. The Pharisees said to him, "Look, why are they doing what is unlawful on the Sabbath?"
>
> He answered, "Have you never read what David did when he and his companions were hungry and in need? In the days of Abiathar the high priest, he entered the house of God and ate the consecrated bread, which is lawful only for priests to eat. And he also gave some to his companions."
>
> Then he said to them, "The Sabbath was made for man, not man for the Sabbath. So the Son of Man is Lord even of the Sabbath."

Jesus' response is important. He is telling us that the Sabbath was meant to be a gift to us. Rest is a blessing to be received, not a burden to be endured.

Just the *Two* of Us

The responsibilities of marriage and family are important and demanding. Take some time together to talk about how you and your spouse might better balance time, rest, and rhythm in your life.

- What pressures do each of you feel that push rest and rhythm out of your life?

- What might you remove from your life that could help to restore balance for you as a couple and as a family?

- How do you think you might practice Sabbath rest in your family life?

Which Will We Choose?

In our foolishness, we go and go and go. The danger is that we miss out on the blessings of time, rest, and rhythm. If we continue our mad dash, we will fall short of experiencing the gift God intended for us to enjoy when he gave us boundaries to deal with the busyness of life.

We are endowed with God's likeness, but we are drastically different in our limitations. God has no need for sleep or slumber. His strength and power know no limits. We get tired. Feel weary. Experience stress. Get overwhelmed. Become distracted. As much as we work, explore, and seek to be ambitious, we are weak and finite in comparison to God, our Creator. The Sabbath is our weekly reminder that God is God and we are not.

The Sabbath can be a difficult gift for those of us living in a culture that values action. We quietly feel condemned or ashamed when we stop to rest from our labor. The slave master in our head cracks the whip if we sit, relax, unwind, or do nothing for too long. It is as if Pharaoh is hissing in our ear, "Get up, do something. There is work to be done. Don't rest. There is too much to do!"

But God's gift of time, rest, and rhythm is one we desperately need to accept and enjoy. The principle of not doing too much, too fast, and too often is especially important for a couple who wants to live out the missing vow with kids in the house. With so much to do, and so many opportunities, how will we cherish the time? How will we guard what is most important? How will we keep our love alive when life is so full?

God invites each of us to steward—wisely and skillfully—the precious time he gives us on this earth. Which will we choose: slavery or freedom? How will we make our days count—in our marriage, in our family, and for the sake of the world?

8

DEALING WITH BUSYNESS

Hurry is the great enemy of spiritual life in our day. You must ruthlessly eliminate hurry from your life.

Dallas Willard

Where are your shoes?" I (*Patrick*) asked Sophia, our youngest daughter. We were running late and hustling down the driveway to our van. She was wearing one purple sock and one pink sock but no shoes. It was October, not June. There was no time to go back into the house to find her shoes. "You'll have to wait to get your shoes until we drop off Tyler and Bella at soccer," I said as authoritatively as I could in the hurried moment to the van. With the emotional understanding of a six-year-old, she burst into tears.

About that time two other events converged. I realized that Cherry, our seven-pound Pomeranian Maltese, was still out on her leash. If the neighbors couldn't hear Sophia crying, it was only because Cherry was barking. The second event? A family from our church stopped by while out riding their bikes. *Perfect*, I thought. *Now I am a bad parent and a bad pastor.* Where was Ruth in all of this? Conveniently out of town.

These are the moments when we just want to hit the "pause" button. Catch our breath. Cool down. Try to make sense of what is happening. Refocus. Start over.

Life with kids in the house comes at us fast. It's rarely neatly packaged. During this season the busy, hurried life is our new normal. The blessings of a life with balance, rest, and rhythm are a distant memory. With so many demands on our time, it is easy for us to lose sight of our purpose as a family and the love we share as a couple.

We can't eliminate the busyness and chaos of life with kids in the house. But we can establish boundaries and make decisions that help to lessen the impact of a hurried life. We can carve out downtime to be refreshed and reenergized as a couple. Stewarding our time well can help us to give our best to each other as we try to live out the missing vow.

How Busy Are We?

When it comes to busyness, most of us feel as if we are running on a treadmill and can't get off. And we aren't afflicted with busyness just because we have kids. Excessive busyness dominates life for most of us. Consider our work life. In an article in *The Atlantic*, research done by economists Dan Hamermesh and Elena Stancanelli shows that Americans are not only working more, but we are bringing work home at night and on the weekends.

On a typical weeknight, a quarter of American workers did some kind of work between 10 p.m. and 6 a.m. That's a lot, compared with about seven percent in France and the Netherlands. The U.K. is closest to the U.S. on this measure, where 19 percent work during night hours. On the weekends, one in three workers in the U.S. were on the job, compared to one in five in France, Germany, and the Netherlands.[1]

What's wrong with working so much? The economists note two setbacks to our hardworking culture: less of a social life and possibly worse health conditions. Hamermesh, for one, says it's not worth it: "We have driven ourselves to the point where we work more and get less and less for it."[2]

We're not just busy working, of course. We're also busy

- taking care of household chores;
- raising children;
- driving to a practice or a game;
- volunteering at church;
- keeping in touch with family and friends.

The question is, what can we do about having too much to do? If our time is limited, and there is less to go around during this season of marriage and family, how do we learn to steward our time? How can we keep busyness from invading our marriage?

---

1. Bourree Lam, "Americans Won't Relax, Even Late at Night or On the Weekend," *The Atlantic* (September 14, 2014), http://www.theatlantic.com/business/archive/2014/09/americans-wont-relax-even-late-at-night-or-on-the-weekend/380146/.
2. Ibid.

What Does Our Busyness Tell Us?

Our busyness may be telling us something about ourselves. So it is important to consider what message might be hidden behind our nonstop activity. Sometimes we can be busy for all the wrong reasons. Taking time to reflect on why we do what we do can help us to understand why our life feels so crowded at times. Gaining an understanding of why we are so busy can help us to protect what is important—our love for our spouse. So consider a few key questions.

Are We Afraid to Say No?

For a variety of reasons, it is sometimes tough to say no. It's not just middle school students who give in to peer pressure. As a couple, or even a family, we can cave in to whatever everyone else is doing. One reason is that we care too much about what other people think. We value their opinion or need their approval. While the Bible encourages us to please people, it warns against people pleasing.

If it is any comfort to you, even Peter, one of the first followers of Jesus, struggled with caving in to the pressure of others. He had to learn the lesson of pleasing God above all others. Why? Paul tells us in Galatians 2:11–14: "He was afraid of those who belonged to the circumcision group" (a Jewish group who believed in Jesus; v. 12). Peter ate with Gentile believers until his fear of other believers, who came to visit, changed his behavior.

Peter acted like an oversized middle school student who didn't want to stick out in the crowd. He feared not belonging, and his fear led him to compromise what he really believed in.

We often do the same. We compromise our values or what we believe in because we fear sticking out or being different. We become people pleasers who are afraid to say no. Sometimes the people we are trying to please are our own kids! We might be afraid to tell them no about playing a sport or engaging in yet another activity.

Other times we may be afraid to say no because we are secretly competing with someone. We are afraid that our kids will fall behind or won't "get in." This fear of failure in competition drives us to engage our children in countless activities. Recently I (*Patrick*) dealt with this kind of fear when making an activity decision for one of our sons.

We were trying to figure out whether a travel league was right for him and for us. I spent nearly an hour on the phone with his coach talking cost, details, and schedules. During the conversation about schedules, I felt the fear creeping in. The schedule seemed excessive for his age. The weekday practices were mandatory, but the Saturday morning practice would be optional. However, the coach told me, "I'll have to reward the players for showing up and working hard." The translation? If your son isn't willing to work as hard as others by coming to all of the practices, I won't play him as often.

Decisions about activities can be difficult for a couple and family to make, because what we say yes to inevitably takes time, energy, and resources from somewhere else. It takes wisdom to discern what is most important and to know when to say no and when to say yes.

As we evaluate our schedule and where we commit our time, we have to ask if our fatigue and busyness are because of our fear of saying no. If so, we need to ask God to give us the wisdom and courage to know what to say no to. Learning to say no to unnecessary or unhealthy activities is one way to say yes to our marriage and family.

Do We Find Too Much Worth in Being Busy?

Sometimes we are too busy not so much out of fear as misplaced worth. All of us are capable of seeking our worth or identity in the wrong things. For some of us it is our success. For others it is our looks. Or perhaps even our stuff. And let's not forget busyness. It can become a source of worth and identity.

Americans highly value ambition, activity, and hard work. While all of these are good, they also have a dark side. Our drive to fit in, keep up, and get ahead leaves couples and families with overly busy schedules, exhaustion, and the loss of unstructured free time. If that isn't enough, doubt about our worth creeps in if we allow ourselves freedom to *not* be busy.

Notice how easily and persistently the busyness and worth myth creeps in to life. Our oldest son loves soccer. At the end of his seventh-grade season, we were talking with another couple when the mom asked, "So what are you going to do this season?"

When we told her "nothing," she looked at us as if we were aliens! "Well, you have to do something, right?"

We have to admit, for a fleeting moment we felt a little "less than." Were we wrong to not have him in something every season? Were we somehow hurting him relationally, athletically, physically, emotionally? It didn't last long, but for a moment we felt as if we had done something wrong.

To rest or not be busy can be perceived as laziness. We get dragged into the rat race because everyone else is doing it. But we don't have to. We don't have to say yes out of fear or to find our worth. It is okay, and we would argue healthy, to learn to say no more often. First John 2:16 says,

> For everything in the world—the lust of the flesh, the lust of the eyes, and the pride of life—comes not from the Father but from the world.

Without God, we need a self-inflated view of ourselves based on our accomplishments, possessions, and busyness. We wrongly believe that all of the activity and achievements validate us. We are not saying all activity is bad. It is, however, dangerous if we are looking to our busyness to define who we are or who our kids are. It also can be hazardous to our marriage and family relationships, which are far more important.

Are We Just Unorganized?

Sometimes it feels as if we are busier than we really are. It's not that we aren't doing anything, but we may be mismanaging our time. Or we might be plain old disorganized.

Time is like money; if we don't budget it, we quickly lose control of it, and it is gone before we know it. We love how Gordon MacDonald describes the principle of budgeting our time: "The disorganized person must have a budgeting perspective. And that means determining the difference between the fixed—what one must do—and the discretionary—what one would like to do."[3]

As hard as we work to live on purpose, the season of life

---

3. Gordon MacDonald, *Ordering Your Private World* (Nashville: Thomas Nelson, 2003), 80.

we are in with kids is hectic. Every week is full of real life. If we aren't diligent in evaluating, choosing, and planning family activities, we will fall victim to rapid-fire demands on our time. Several years ago, in an effort to gain the upper hand in managing our time, Ruth suggested that we start keeping a weekly and monthly family calendar. It is one of the best things we have done for our family and our marriage. We don't know why it took us so long to figure it out.

We start by scheduling the must-dos—what Gordon MacDonald would call the "fixed" appointments and activities. Then we begin scheduling the "discretionary" activities, the things we would like to do. Having it all on paper helps us to evaluate what is most important and what we need to say no to. The family calendar helps us to live with greater purpose and focus. A schedule allows us to integrate our different roles and activities into a daily rhythm.

The next challenge, of course, is to make every effort to execute the plan. That part still has room for improvement! But at least the schedule gives us structure and a goal to shoot for. I (*Patrick*) sync our weekly and monthly schedule with my work schedule. This allows Ruth and me to be on the same page with activities and commitments. It's not always perfect, but at least it's a plan.

Busyness is inevitable during the season of marriage with kids in the house. So we need to be aware of why we are busy so we can determine whether we need to be busy with certain activities and commitments. We don't want to be busy for the wrong reasons. The goal is to carve out time so we don't become too busy for each other. We want to protect our love for each other.

Redeem the Time We *Do* Have

"How in the world did it get to be 11:00 p.m. already?" Ruth asked me. We had just gotten all of the kids in bed, the dogs walked, and the laundry done. We had been looking forward to some alone time. But our day was basically over. So much for sitting in the library together watching football. Our alone time had disappeared—again.

When life is moving fast, it's easy to focus on the time we don't have. But when we focus on what we don't have, we can overlook the moments that are right under our nose. We are learning to make the most of those bits of time we have alone. Just recently, our kids were playing at a friend's house. We knew we had about an hour to ourselves. It was tempting to use that precious time to catch up on email, clean, or tackle some of the other things that needed doing. Instead, we went for a walk. A nice, quiet walk together.

Sometimes redeeming the time we have means sneaking out for a lunch date, enjoying coffee together in the morning, running to the grocery store together, or conversing over a cup of tea at night. These brief moments are really rather ordinary, but they become significant moments when we share them together.

Time does not come to us wrapped in a nice, neat package. Our gifts of time for each other are not always flashy or romantic. Time often shows up unannounced, in scattered moments. So we do our best to take advantage of the little moments God gives us to cultivate and nurture our marriage. We may not have much when it comes to time together, but how we use what we have matters a lot.

Living with Limits

Okay, this is a tough one! One of the reasons we become overwhelmed with busyness is because we have so many opportunities available to us as a couple, as children, and as a family. With so many choices clamoring for our involvement, it can be hard to set limits and live with them—especially when you love the options.

Consider just one area of options—our children's activities. When I (*Patrick*) grew up, we played backyard football, basketball in the driveway, and Wiffle ball in the street. Our "travel league" was riding our bikes around the neighborhood until we recruited enough kids to have two teams. It's not like that today.

Children have far more sports and extracurricular activities available to them. When I first started in ministry, it was almost unheard of to have activities on a Wednesday night or Sunday. That's just not the case anymore. There is no such thing as a day that is off-limits. The travel, schedule, and expenses of many activities increasingly demand more commitment from families.

Travel leagues, for example, have become increasingly popular—and pricey! (We thought braces were going to be the major expense!) A couple can spend thousands of dollars for just one child to play one sport, and this does not include gas, lodging, and food expenses. I (*Patrick*) nearly failed math in high school, but even I can crunch the numbers and figure out that's a lot of money, especially if there are multiple children in the house.

No matter what activities our children are involved in, an overcommitted schedule can easily squeeze out any time to cultivate a vibrant, God-honoring marriage. This is especially true when several kids are involved in multiple activities at the same time. Deciding to live within limits means we have to take a hard look at the cost, sacrifice, impact on our marriage and the rest of the family, and the fruit of certain opportunities and activities.

As a couple with kids who are getting older, we are trying to navigate some of the tough decisions about sports and activities. We've wrestled with some hard questions, wondering if we are trying to do too much for our kids or if we're not giving them enough. We've weighed the cost and asked, Is it worth it? We've considered God's purpose for marriage and family and asked, Are we doing the right thing?

For example, our kids love sports, so working through which and how many is a challenge. For the good of our kids, our family, and our marriage, we have limited the number of sports our kids play in a year. If each of our four kids were playing multiple sports throughout the year, it would be too time-consuming for us as a couple and as a family. We have set the expectation with them that when they get into sixth grade, they have to choose one sport to play that year. Considering our kids' additional involvement in music lessons and church activities, this has made for a healthy balance for all of us.

Every couple with kids has to use wisdom to protect their marriage and family from an overcommitted schedule. It is critical that we, as parents, set the pace and the limits for our kids and not the other way around. Choosing to live within limitations means choosing to say no to some things. It's okay to limit the number of opportunities children can participate in during a year. It just might be the best thing for them and the best thing for protecting our marriage.

Just the *Two* of Us

We can't escape busyness, but we can navigate it in a more healthy way. Take time together to talk about ways you might do a better job of guarding your marriage during this busy season of life.

- Which of the reasons for busyness did you most recognize in yourself?
- What impact do you think busyness is having on your relationship with your spouse, and how could you better protect it?
- What "limits" do you think would be most beneficial to your marriage and family?

Protect What Matters Most

In our efforts to limit the busyness of life, we need to be careful. We sometimes overreact and err too far in the other direction. Protecting our time doesn't mean becoming greedy with it. It doesn't mean we guard our time at the expense of investing it in others. Signs that we are guarding our time too closely might be when we no longer serve in our church, invite friends into our home, or reach out to neighbors. This misuse of our time prevents us from loving and being loved the way Jesus intended.

Protecting our time isn't just about what we do or don't do; it means living more proactively rather than reactively. It means living on purpose, with an eye on God's eternal purposes for our marriage and family. It means creating a rhythm to life that is based on the convictions and values that guide us. Our convictions and values help inform our decisions and provide the criteria we use for saying yes or no. They help us know how to protect whatever precious time we have as a couple or family.

Jesus constantly faced the pressure of people and the passing of time. With limited time and unlimited needs on earth, he had to protect what mattered most: his mission. Jesus didn't heal every disease, respond to every question, satisfy every need, or even visit every town. He measured all that he did against the mission his Father gave to him.

For us it has been helpful to write down our core values and convictions for life as a family. This short, simple list helps keep in focus our mission as a married couple with kids. It helps us know how to establish a rhythm for life—how to arrange our time and activities in a way that protects what is most important. These values may change depending on what season we are in and what ages our kids are. Consider a few core rhythms that we hold on to during this season of our life:

- We value being together by eating together.
- We intentionally live within limits.
- We have fun together.
- We practice family devotions to pass on our faith.
- We value learning and exploring.
- We strive to be healthy in what we eat, how we play, and the way we live.
- We engage in ministry *as* a family, not just ministry *to* our family.

Just the *Two* of Us

Take some time out to prayerfully talk about what is most important for you and your spouse to protect during this season of life.

- Which core convictions and values set the rhythm of life for you as a couple and as a family?

- Which additional convictions and values are needed to protect your marriage during this season of marriage with kids?

Write down your top three to five convictions so that you can refer to them as you make decisions to establish protective rhythms for your life.

Slowing Down for Rest

Getting away and finding rest is not easy. Disconnecting takes effort. We encounter all kinds of obstacles when we try to shut down the busyness.

We know the Bible says to "love your neighbor," but on occasion we found ourselves hiding from a highly extroverted neighbor. Personal space did not exist for this person. One day I (*Patrick*) had a few minutes to myself. Exhausted, I fell asleep on our couch.

I didn't sleep long. A light tapping noise on our window woke me up. At first I thought it might be one of the kids. Then I thought it might be a bird. Perhaps it was a branch, being gently tossed back and forth by the wind. Nope. Those options vanished when my weary eyes focused enough to see my neighbor peeking into our house! He saw me sleeping but was not inclined to let me enjoy the moment.

No matter how hard we try, chances are good we can't simply pick a day (or even a few minutes) and disappear from the world. That doesn't mean we give up on slowing down and finding rest. We can still apply the principle of Sabbath rest—making rest a part of the rhythm of life—to our lives. Your family needs may make setting apart a Saturday or Sunday for rest impossible. If so, pick another day or time that works for you.

Rest can be a part of life even when you can't get away physically. Time alone can be as simple as disconnecting from other people (especially the distractions of social media), activities, and work. It can actually be a relief to say no to phones, Facebook, Twitter, and Instagram for a period of time. Maybe we slow down by occasionally saying no to having friends over on a particular evening. As families and couples, we need time "away" to refuel and refocus on one another.

Most important, rest from the busyness of life is not found in what we do or don't do. Let's not lose sight of the fact that rest is ultimately found in a person, Jesus. The real place to settle our soul and find rest is not in identifying the right priorities, practicing the right disciplines, or establishing the perfect rhythm. Real and lasting rest for our soul is found by staying close to Jesus. Psalm 62:1–2 describes true rest this way:

> Truly my soul finds rest in God;
>   my salvation comes from him.

> Truly he is my rock and my salvation;
> he is my fortress, I will never be shaken.

And in Matthew 11:28, Jesus says, "Come to me, all you who are weary and burdened, and I will give you rest."

So be wise as you learn to balance the busy. Live on purpose. Seek to say yes to what is best. Avoid letting the craziness of this season in life pull you apart as a couple. But above everything, pursue Jesus. Let his Word and his promises encourage and strengthen you.

9

WHEN YOU'RE RUNNING ON EMPTY

Though one may be overpowered, two can defend themselves.

Ecclesiastes 4:12

I (*Patrick*) have a bit of a reputation for running out of gas, perhaps because I once read an article that said gas pumps have more germs than a toilet seat. I don't know how many germs that is, but it's enough for me not to want to touch either one too often. Or maybe it's because it takes time to slow down, stop, and fill up. Whatever the reason, I don't enjoy stopping for gas, which is why I run out so often.

Some experts say you can drive your car at least forty miles after your gas light comes on. My "research" would say that is fairly accurate—some cars more and others less. Normal people pull over and refuel long before the warning light comes on, but not me. I once pushed my motorcycle beyond the forty-mile test limit. I lost—again. If anything has come close to motivating me to change my ways, it was walking my Harley for just over a mile through our neighborhood and past our neighbor who hates Harleys and loves Yamahas. Exhausting and embarrassing!

Parenting Is a Gas Guzzler

Any way you look at it, parenting is a gas guzzler. Surviving the transition from married couple to married with kids requires a lot of energy. Living out God's purpose for marriage and family is exhausting. Trying to do it well often leaves us running on empty. One of the biggest reasons we find ourselves running low on fuel is because of self-neglect.

We all believe that good parents are selfless parents. When kids come along, we often neglect or set aside what we want and need for the sake of our children. It is easy to get into a pattern of self-sacrifice and self-neglect that ultimately leads to spouse neglect:

- We say good-bye to hobbies or interests we once enjoyed.
- We sacrifice sleep.
- We stop exercising.
- We drive more.
- We talk less.
- We eat last and quickly. Sitting down is optional.

We go and we give and then we do it all over again! Receiving feels like a luxury. For all of these reasons and more, we run low on fuel. It comes with the territory.

Warning Signs of Self-Neglect

Unfortunately we don't have a "running on empty" light like most vehicles. So self-neglect is not always easy to spot or admit. It is helpful if we are aware of and watch for some of the warning signs of running on empty:

- Sustained feelings of being overwhelmed by normal tasks
- Loss of joy and excitement
- A diminished romantic life
- Being easily irritated, always feeling "on edge"
- Sensing a lack of peace or being "unsettled" in your soul
- Feeling overly anxious
- Unresolved bitterness or resentment
- Frequent illness or chronic health issues
- Lacking enthusiasm for activities you once enjoyed
- Feeling drained, burned out, or unusually tired

We understand that there may be causes for these feelings other than self-neglect. If that is the case, seeking the counsel of a physician, Christian counselor, or pastor is critical.

Every couple knows what it feels like to run on empty. But if continued, self-neglect will eventually stop us in our tracks. You can drive on fumes for only so long! Trust me, I know.

The dangers of self-sacrifice and self-neglect may seem

innocent or harmless at first. But if we stay in that place for too long, we begin to lose energy, zeal, and passion for everything in life. We become so fatigued and low on fuel that every little thing becomes a challenge. Just the thought of a normal, simple task like loading the dishwasher (again) feels like climbing a mountain! Innocent comments set us off. When self-neglect continues and everything feels like a challenge, we almost always run out of energy for our marriage too.

We don't have the energy to surprise our spouse anymore. We don't pursue each other romantically like we used to. Relational intimacy is too much effort after a long day of work and parenting. We stop listening. Talking gets harder. The energy for each other is gone. Loving our spouse with kids in the house becomes an enormous task because our energy has been so depleted giving to our kids that we don't have much left. There's little, if anything, left to give to our spouse. Sustained self-neglect eventually leads to sacrifice, and the sacrifice is usually our spouse.

Self-neglect is dangerous not only because it steals our energy but because it becomes a convenient distraction or excuse to ignore important relational needs and concerns. Under pressure, self-neglect forces our marriage to take a backseat. "I just want to focus on getting the kids through this year," one wife told me. In the middle of a hectic time, a husband said, "I don't have time to be thinking about what she wants too!"

We all have legitimate activities and circumstances that demand a lot of us. But we need to be careful that self-neglect and self-sacrifice for the sake of our kids does not become an excuse for spouse-neglect as well. We need to guard against allowing resentment to build up between us because of poor communication or conflicts that get ignored or minimized. All of these "gas guzzlers" can leave us depleted and distant in our most important human relationship.

Watch Each Other's Back

A marriage that is healthy when kids are in the house is a marriage in which each spouse protects the other. On our own, we are easily overpowered. We run out of fuel. But when we are watchful of each other, when we have each other's back, we can recognize when our spouse is dangerously low on fuel. We can then step in to help our spouse refuel by providing much-needed love, respect, attention, and support.

For example, not long ago, Patrick was having a particularly trying week. He is usually the one who gets up and takes our two dogs for their morning walks. Knowing he had a lot on his mind and schedule, I got up and took care of the dogs. While it might not seem like a lot, I knew that taking care of this for Patrick would ease some of the heavy load he was carrying.

Protecting each other should not be just an emergency maneuver. Protecting each other needs to be proactive and preventive and persistent (meaning you try to fill each other's tank a little bit every day!). For example, you can protect each other by:

- making sure they get a good night's sleep;
- providing a healthy, balanced meal;
- allowing time for exercise;
- being extra tender during an illness;

- supporting their time with friends;
- taking on a household chore;
- letting them just relax;
- challenging them to say no;
- making love;
- offering an encouraging word;
- listening to their dreams, goals, or everyday details;
- praying for them.

As we seek to live out the missing vow in our marriage, we have to remember to cherish and protect each other. God has given each of us a gift—a spouse who provides love, protection, and support when the demands of life leave us running on empty, and a spouse who needs that from us as well.

Don't Turn on Each Other!

One of the classic battlefield bloopers is recorded in the Old Testament book of Judges. I (*Patrick*) like to read this passage at weddings to remind couples that marriage is both a blessing and a covenant relationship in which we have to have each other's back. In this story, enemies of Israel, the Midianites, made a tragic mistake by failing to protect one another.

To give a little background, the story is about God giving Israel victory over the Midianites. God's battle plan first required Gideon to trim his army down to three hundred men. God did not want Israel to take credit for overwhelming the Midianites by their own strength, so he made sure they knew they were weak. Next, God instructed Gideon to arm his strike force with nothing more than clay jars, torches, and trumpets. Gideon's army then split into three companies of a hundred men each and surrounded the Midianites for a surprise attack. What odds would you place on their success?

In the dead of night, while the Midianites were sleeping, Gideon's army approached the camp. At Gideon's command, all of his men smashed their jars, raised their torches, blew their trumpets, and shouted out in surprise:

> "A sword for the LORD and for Gideon!" While each man held his position around the camp, all the Midianites ran, crying out as they fled. When the three hundred trumpets sounded, the LORD caused the men throughout the camp to turn on each other with their swords. (Judges 7:20–22)

Who hasn't been jolted out of a sound sleep by a crying baby or a barking dog? Imagine being awakened by three hundred trumpets and smashing jars! We would cry too! In a moment of confusion, stress, disorientation, and chaos, the Midianites misunderstood who the enemy was. They turned on themselves, defeating one another, instead of protecting one another.

Why do I like this passage when talking about marriage? There is no reason, apart from God's supernatural intervention, that the Midianites should not have been able to protect themselves. But instead of protecting one another and fighting for one another, the Midianites turned against one another. All too often the same thing happens in marriage.

With all of the self-neglect, stress, and busyness of marriage with kids in the house, we too can fall into the trap. We defeat ourselves by turning against each other instead of protecting each other. If we are going to live out the missing vow of loving our spouse with kids in the house, we have to have each other's back. Fight the enemies out there, not the spouse who sleeps beside you!

Protecting Each Other by Carrying Each Other's Burdens

Marriage and parenting is exhausting—like running-a-marathon exhausting! Most couples who have been running on self-neglect for too long feel weary. So the encouragement in Galatians 6:2 to "carry each other's burdens, and in this way you will fulfill the law of Christ" is a key principle for protecting each other during the season of being married with kids.

The Greek word translated as "carry" means to "put upon one's self, to lift up, or carry what is burdensome." It conveys the idea of coming alongside and lightening the load for another person. When we carry another's burden, we take that burden on ourselves. We share the load so that the other person doesn't suffer alone.

Dietrich Bonhoeffer, a German pastor and theologian who spoke out boldly against Hitler, wrote that Christians "must bear the burden of a brother. He must suffer and endure the brother. It is only when he is a burden that another person is really a brother and not merely an object to be manipulated."[1]

Bonhoeffer was saying that relationships in the real world, especially Christian relationships, come with responsibility. Jesus calls us to do some heavy lifting for one another.

---

1. Dietrich Bonhoeffer, *Life Together: The Classic Exploration of Christian in Community* (New York: Harper One, 2009), 100.

Marriage in particular comes with a charge to "carry each other's burdens." Our spouse is not "an object to be manipulated"; rather we are called to "endure" and even "suffer" for and with each other.

That is a convicting statement! We might not come out and say we see our spouse as "an object to be manipulated," but how often do we look to get something *from* our spouse instead of looking out *for* our spouse? Protecting our spouse requires that we provide strength when our spouse is weak or struggling. One way we can love our spouse is by attempting to lighten the load when our spouse is running on empty.

Just the Two of Us

We were not meant to carry the burdens of parenting—discipline, scheduling, finances, schoolwork—alone. Take a few minutes to talk about ways you and your spouse need each other to help carry the load.

- In which areas of marriage or parenting are you struggling right now?
- In what ways do you need your spouse to come alongside and help carry the burden for you?
- What specific things can you do to help your spouse carry the burden and avoid self-neglect?

Sometimes the Small Stuff
Is the Big Stuff

I could tell Ruth was living in another world. She was home, but not home. Our lives had accelerated from crazy to crazier when we were given the opportunity to write two books (*Hoodwinked* and *For Better or for Kids*). We had already been trying to balance our pastoral ministry, schooling our four kids, two online ministries (*The Better Mom* and *For the Family*), and then . . . two books?! The thought did occur to us to run away to a cabin in northern Michigan and ask God to send someone else.

We were both feeling a bit overwhelmed. Ruth was especially feeling the weight of all God had put in front of us. So as I headed out to work one day, I simply said, "You're feeling spent, aren't you?"

That's all it took. What followed was a whole lot of tears— the I-am-going-to-have-to-change-my-shirt kind of tears.

"What can I do?" I asked. "If this is what God has for us right now, we need to make some adjustments. We can't live like this for too long. What can I do to help you?"

I wish I could say I am always this gracious, but that would be lying. However, at that moment God graciously gave me the eyes to see that I needed to have Ruth's back. She was running dangerously low on gas. There was no way we were headed toward a good ending with the kind of self-neglect we were experiencing. A burden needed to be carried.

So we had some difficult, but good, discussions. We made adjustments. We worked out ways to work together and help to carry each other's burdens.

One decision was that on my day off (Fridays), Ruth would get away, undistracted and uninterrupted, to write, respond to emails, and manage the sites. It was time set apart for her to do what she needed to do. I, in turn, would take care of things on the home front. Done. Easy solution. Just knowing that she would have one day every week to do what she needed to do was a lifesaver for Ruth. It brought focus and fuel when she was feeling preoccupied and drained.

Sometimes it's not always big stuff that we need to protect. It can be hundreds of little—small, simple, and easy— things we can do to lighten the load and help each other refuel, such as:

- making coffee;
- doing the dishes;
- taking the kids to the park;
- folding the laundry (and putting it away!);
- taking out the garbage;
- giving the kids a bath;
- shoveling the driveway;
- mowing the grass.

All of these simple everyday tasks, done with an attitude of loving service toward each other, help fight fatigue. They help to fill an empty fuel tank. They recharge and renew us when the responsibilities of marriage and family become a burden.

Rest Area Ahead!

When we take a road trip, we almost always judge pit stops by whether or not there is a Starbucks. It's the perfect combination. We refuel the car and refuel ourselves with caffeine (which inevitably leads to additional rest stops for, shall we say, relief). Major highways and especially interstates always tell us well in advance how many miles we have left before we reach the next rest stop or exit. These signs let us pace ourselves, telling us when and where to go.

Parenting doesn't come with designated rest areas or signs that direct us to refueling stops. God designed the job of parenting to come with an intimate partner who joins us on the journey, who watches our back and protects us from running on empty. So what are some practical ways we can help to protect each other from the dangers of self-neglect? How can we know for sure if we are providing the fuel our spouse really needs? Here are a few specific ways we can bring rest and relief to each other.

Learn to Listen to Each Other's Hearts

The Bible reveals a God who not only speaks but listens. He stops. He hears. He turns his affection toward us by turning his attention toward us. The Hebrew poets describe the impact of God's listening love in various ways:

> For what other nation is so great as to have their gods near them the way the LORD our God is near to us whenever we pray to him? (Deuteronomy 4:7)

I waited patiently for the LORD; he turned to me and heard my cry. (Psalm 40:1)

I love the LORD, for he heard my voice; he heard my cry for mercy. Because he turned his ear to me, I will call on him as long as I live. (Psalm 116:1–2)

God loves by listening. This is what God does for us. As Dietrich Bonhoeffer says, "It is God's love for us that He not only gives us His Word, but also lends us His ear."[2]

We may not think of listening as an act of love, but it is. God desires for us to not only speak to each other in love but to listen to each other in love. When we turn our ear toward our spouse, we are also turning our heart in love toward our spouse. We are attempting to deeply understand the words our spouse is saying.

When we're caught in the rush of life with kids in the house, we need to learn to use our ears to draw our hearts closer to each other. This requires us to slow down long enough to find out what is really going on with our spouse. By listening, we can discover how our spouse is really doing, where the greatest struggles are, and whether our spouse feels loved and respected in the midst of all the turmoil.

Seek God Together

There can be a lot of stress, anxiety, busyness, and fear in marriage and parenting. When those emotions are present within us, we often cling to Psalm 94:19: "When anxiety was great within me, your consolation brought me joy." The

---

2. Bonhoeffer, *Life Together*, 97.

psalmist reminds us that there is a power greater than our-selves available to us. That power is God's Word.

Like a little child, we need to be consoled with God's truth, power, and the hope of his promises. His Word is the "bread" we can live on. We can count on it to sustain us. We need "every word that comes from the mouth of God" (Matthew 4:4) to give us joy, rest, and peace when we are running on empty.

As a couple, we protect each other as we share the pro-vision of God's life-giving Word. Looking at God's Word together helps us to stay centered. It keeps us focused on the right kind of marriage and the right mission. It gives us direction as we move forward in our marriage and as parents. We refresh and renew each other as we seek God's wisdom together.

Share Words That Keep You Going

Our words carry great power. They can heal or hurt. They truly do possess the potential for life or death (Proverbs 18:21). One of our favorite verses about our words reads, "The tongue that brings healing is a tree of life" (Proverbs 15:4 [1984 NIV]). As a couple, we want our words to bring life to each other.

Sometimes it takes only a word of truth, praise, or encour-agement to preserve life for our spouse. All day long, energy is being drained from us. We get emotionally and spiritually beat up just from the daily process of life—working to provide for our family, sacrificing our needs for our family, and dealing with everyday stress. We take hits from the outside, but we also take hits from the inside. We sometimes experience men-tal and emotional fatigue because we believe the ever-present lies about who we are as a husband, father, wife, or mother. Whenever we feel insecure or inadequate, we burn more fuel.

We face enough adversaries in life (and we don't mean our children). What we need in each other is an advocate who restores us with words of life and healing. Our words can be a great source of rest, strength, and power to keep us both going.

Pray When Your Spouse Needs More Than You Can Provide

Sometimes our spouse will face challenges that are just too big for us to help with—challenges that are beyond our wisdom, resources, or strength. This was true for us several years ago. We had moved from a church and friends we had known for ten years. We were walking through a new and difficult ministry season—unlike anything we had been through before. Then, in the span of just two years, Patrick lost both of his parents.

Stressful would be an understatement! During that time, I (*Ruth*) was helpless when it came to enabling Patrick to refuel. I wanted to help, but I didn't know what I could do or how to do it. Patrick needed Someone bigger than me.

So I did the best thing I could do. I prayed often and hard for him. We were in too deep, way over our heads! We had come to the end of ourselves, and God alone could provide what we needed.

As a couple, one of the greatest things we can do to protect and refuel each other is to pray often. It is a great gift to be able to take each other before God's throne and say, "We can't do this on our own. God, we don't have the wisdom. We need you. We are wiped out, exhausted, running on empty. We need you to strengthen us. Help us find the joy, the strength, and the wisdom to keep pressing on."

Am I Loving You the Way You Need Me To?

In marriage, our love for each other makes all the difference when we are at risk of running on empty. A spouse who knows us, loves us, and is watching our back may be the first to know that we need to slow down and refuel. A loving spouse can provide support, refreshment, and encouragement when the demands of life with kids in the house leave us empty. But it takes intentional effort to love our spouse as God intends.

When Jesus said the second greatest commandment was to "love your neighbor as yourself" (Matthew 19:19; Mark 12:31; Luke 10:27), he meant more than your next-door neighbor. He also meant those we live closest to—our spouse! Paul emphasizes the importance of loving your spouse: "Each one of you also must love his wife as he loves himself, and the wife must respect her husband" (Ephesians 5:33).

What might be the difference between loving your neighbor as yourself and loving your spouse as yourself? One thought is that in marriage our life-giving love and concern for each other is not always demonstrated as overtly as it is in other relationships. We tend to make assumptions regarding our love for our spouse and sometimes gloss over or even ignore the need to express it. So the extra emphasis on loving our spouse is meant to be a subtle reminder that our sacred covenant in marriage must be highly valued and that protecting our spouse must be a high priority.

How do you know if you're loving your spouse properly? One rabbi had a clever answer. The "real proof," says Professor Reuven Kimelman of whether you have fulfilled this command, "is not whether *you* feel you have fulfilled it, but whether your wife feels that you love her as you love yourself."[3]

When we love our spouse as we love ourselves, we will make the effort to stay close together. We will remember to love one another by having each other's back, always ready to offer protection, a helping hand, an encouraging word. Regardless of the circumstances we face in life, we can face them together.

3. Rabbi Joseph Telushkin, *Jewish Wisdom: Ethical, Spiritual, and Historical Lessons from the Great Works and Thinkers* (New York: William Morrow, 1994), 125.

10

COMMUNICATING IN THE CHAOS

For the mouth speaks what the heart is full of.
Luke 6:45

We were in college when we had one of our first communication problems. Little did we know it would be a picture of what was to come after we would get married, have kids, and try to find time to actually connect with each other. I had called Ruth after work one night. I was in Indiana, she was in Michigan. I hadn't yet bought a cell phone, so we were still using what seems like an archaic form of communication today—a landline phone.

Midway through our conversation, a summer storm blew in. Like most storms, it started slowly and became more intense and more ominous the longer it lingered. Before long, our conversation became choppy because of static—lots of static. All we could hear of our conversation was a little snippet here and a little snippet there.

As the lightning and thunder increased, our phone call became nothing but fragments, broken sentences, and interruptions. The interference was too much to carry on a meaningful conversation. So, a little frustrated and disappointed, we resigned ourselves to talking later.

Our communication problem was not relational. We weren't fighting or having a disagreement. Our broken communication wasn't about what was happening between us, but what was happening around us. External circumstances simply began to disrupt our connection to the point we could no longer communicate effectively. We would soon learn that being married with kids would do the same.

If you have been married for any length of time, you know that communicating can be difficult. Add a few kids to the mix, and communication becomes more challenging, complex, and sometimes (ahem . . . a lot of the time) chaotic! Verbal interaction between a husband and a wife can become a lot like that summer phone call. And those "external forces" are our own flesh and blood! They are the precious kids we brought into the world, the ones we love and treasure. But kids have an impact on communication.

The loss of communication in marriage can create distance, a lack of intimacy, frustration, resentment, and in worst-case scenarios, the loss of relationship altogether. So cultivating communication in the midst of family chaos is essential if we are to fulfill the missing vow.

Talking Fuels Relationship

Recently, I (*Patrick*) was busted.

It wasn't what I was caught with; it was what I was caught without—the information Ruth had just shared with me.

I started out strong. Ruth was giving me dates for when she was going to be out of town. She told me who was coming to watch the kids while I was at work, what we would eat, and basically, her plan to ensure our survival during her absence.

I knew what she was saying was important, but hearing her wasn't easy. She had a lot of competition. Noah, our youngest son, was asking me to watch him attempt one-arm push-ups. I could hear what sounded like a storm brewing upstairs as our girls "discussed" what happened to the hairbrush. And the dog, the one that barks at every human being who walks by our house, was—you guessed it—barking.

I was trying really hard to listen, but apparently not hard enough. It was a slow fade, just enough to lose our connection. Eventually, I noticed Ruth's body language. We had reached a point in our discussion that required my response. As I fumbled to piece together enough of what I had heard, it became clear I was in trouble!

"You weren't listening, were you?" she asked. I was busted. After almost seventeen years of marriage, I've learned that a good defense is no defense at all. A straight up admission of guilt was all I had to offer.

Sometimes it takes real effort for a couple to talk and listen to each other. And apparently there is no substitute for talking when it comes to two people building a connection. An article in the *New York Times* called "To Fall in Love with Anyone, Do This" caught our attention.[1] The main premise of the article is that two strangers who sit down and ask each other increasingly personal questions will find love. An experiment done by

---

1. Mandy Len Catron, "To Fall in Love with Anyone, Do This," *New York Times* (January 9, 2015), http://www.nytimes.com/2015/01/11/fashion/modern-love-to-fall-in-love-with-anyone-do-this.html.

psychologist Arthur Aron nearly twenty years ago consisted of thirty-six questions that two strangers ask each other. What was the outcome of their increasingly personal conversation? It was the birth of intimate love between two people who previously were unknown to each other. Apparently the original couple in the study found love after only six months.

We're not suggesting that this is the way people should fall in love. However, the article illustrates what the Bible teaches about intimacy: intimacy is created and cultivated through the sharing of information.

Intimacy grows in the fertile soil of face time, when a husband and wife spend time together. Intimacy grows as a couple talk about their dreams, fears, successes, failures, or even just their day. By talking about the stuff of life, we unpack our heart for another to know, love, and treasure. This is what makes love scary. Intimacy is a deep understanding of each other—the good, bad, and ugly.

We found this to be true in the early years of dating and marriage. When we spent time together, we talked about anything and everything. Some of the things we talked about were quite ridiculous, like eye color. Some were mundane, like the homework we were working on. Some were silly, like when we shared our most embarrassing moments. And of course some were serious—discussions of our family background, our worst fears, our greatest dreams, and our spiritual questions.

You name it; we talked about it. It wasn't fancy or overly romantic. It was simply two people learning about each other and sharing with each other who they were. By talking, we came to know and love virtually everything about each other. Intimacy was being birthed through information. Communication was fanning the flame for real and lasting love to flourish.

No relationship sustains that kind of intense communication, but no relationship can survive without continued intimate communication. While some of the emotions of the "honeymoon phase" of communication may fade, a couple has to be careful not to cease talking in personal, intimate ways. If we don't fuel the flames of intimacy, one or both of us will begin to feel distant and isolated. In the absence of intimacy is isolation.

Talk about Talking

A study done several years ago found that married couples tend to overestimate how much they really communicate with each other. The study found that in some cases, "spouses communicate no better than strangers."[2] In light of this, the researchers coined the phrase "closeness-communication bias" to describe our tendency to think that we talk more than we actually do.

One of the researchers observed that "some couples may indeed be on the same wavelength, but maybe not as much as they think. You get rushed and preoccupied, and you stop taking the perspective of the other person, precisely because the two of you are so close."[3] The result is that those couples who think they are communicating have an "illusion" of intimacy. Even though they may be communicating, they are not as close as they think they are.

2. William Harms, "Couples Sometimes Communicate No Better than Strangers," *UChicago News* (January 20, 2011), http://news.uchicago.edu/article/2011/01/20/couples-sometimes-communicate-no-better-strangers-study-finds.
3. Ibid.

Surviving the Shift

When kids come along, couples experience a "shift of inti-macy." A husband and wife are no longer the center of their relationship. A spouse is now sharing time, attention, and affection with children. This is not bad, but it is dangerous when it becomes a barrier to the sharing of life that a couple once enjoyed.

I (*Patrick*) was alone in my office. Ruth was at home in the backyard with our four kids and a few of their friends. I wanted to talk. After a few failed attempts to have a conver-sation without interruptions, I gave up. It was obvious that I was not the center of attention, so I let Ruth know it. I threw an adult-sized temper tantrum and abandoned the mission of talking. "Forget it," I finally said. "I'll just call you later."

Opportunities to know and be known by our spouse can take a backseat when kids enter the picture. Words shared with a spouse can become scarce, often snuffed out by busyness, cri-ses, and exhaustion. Quiet time to simply be together may be nearly impossible. So one of the challenges a couple encounters when kids enter the house is to find ways to continue sharing life together by exchanging simple information and seemingly insignificant details of our day. Our words join us together, little by little building safe and sacred bonds of intimacy.

Our Words Belong to God

Our words did not begin with us; they began with God. The Creator of heaven and earth has chosen not to be silent. Nine times in Genesis 1 we read, "God said . . ." God is the author of words: he communicates and builds intimacy with his creation through the words he speaks.

God wired us for communication because of who he is. He speaks to reveal himself to us. He lets us in, inviting us to join him on a journey. He opens the door not only to his story but also to his heart. When God speaks, he does so with goodness, love, creativity, and beauty. Life rolls off his tongue.

But not all words bring life. Satan uses words too. Unlike the words of God, Satan's words bring doubt, death, pain, separation, and ultimately, the loss of paradise.

Given the conflict between God's words and Satan's words, it is not surprising that the first married couple, the husband and wife God brought together in the garden, would have a breakdown in communication. At a crucial juncture, Adam failed to speak:

> When the woman saw that the fruit of the tree was good for food and pleasing to the eye, and also desirable for gaining wisdom, she took some and ate it. She also gave some to her husband, who was with her, and he ate it. (Genesis 3:6)

Adam was not in some far corner of the garden fetching firewood or taking a nap. He was with the woman. He was close enough and aware enough to say, "No!" He could have used his words to fight off evil and protect his wife, but he didn't. Instead, Adam was speechless.

Adam doesn't stay quiet for long, however. When God comes looking for him, he opens his mouth to speak and fumbles again. This time he uses words to blame his wife: "The woman you put here with me—she gave me some fruit from the tree, and I ate it" (Genesis 3:12). Instead of taking responsibility, Adam shifts the blame to God and his wife. The downward spiral continues as Eve shifts the blame to the serpent: "The serpent deceived me, and I ate" (Genesis 3:13). She, like Adam, opts out of taking responsibility and uses her words to accuse someone else.

What a mess of words! Kids haven't even come on the scene and the first couple, clothed as image bearers of the God who speaks, use their words against each other instead of for each other. Like so many who have come after them, they use words to blame, accuse, hurt, escape, and avoid. Their struggle with communication is a humbling reminder of how important our words really are. As image bearers of God, our words are meant to reflect God's love. How are we using the words we share with our spouse?

Just the *Two* of Us

Take some time to talk about ways your communication could be improved for more intimate conversation between you and your spouse.

- Which changes do you and your spouse most need to make in how you communicate?
- How do you think improving your communication could change your marriage?
- How could allowing God to change the desires of your heart impact the communication between you and your spouse?

Will We Choose Words of Life or Death?

A couple in our neighborhood seemed to be yelling their way through marriage and parenting. Everyone in the neighborhood knew it except for them. If their kids were across the street, they yelled for them to come home. If they were in our backyard, they yelled. And when one of their sons did something wrong—yep, more yelling.

Sometimes we would hear them yell at each other. Now I realize that having kids in the house amps up communication. But yelling at everything can't possibly bring life. It sure didn't for us. Even Ginger, our hamster, flinched a little when they yelled.

Words are not weaklings. Communication comes with tremendous power. According to Proverbs 18:21, the way we wield our tongues—the words we use—will bring either life or death. Notice the power for life and joy that comes from using our communication to bring glory to God:

> Gold there is, and rubies in abundance,
>> but lips that speak knowledge are a rare jewel.
>> (Proverbs 20:15)

> Anxiety weighs down the heart,
>> but a kind word cheers it up. (Proverbs 12:25)

> The lips of the righteous nourish many,
>> but fools die for lack of sense. (Proverbs 10:21)

Lips that speak life are like gold and rare jewels. Life is full of stress and anxiety, but the right words are like medicine. They soothe, resurrect, and bring cheer when there is discouragement. Choice words, like good food, bring health and sustenance. They produce well-being. Which kind of words do we want to bring to our spouse?

Our Words Reveal Who We Are

Have you ever had one of those moments as a couple when you thought no one else was listening? When you thought it was safe to talk because the kids were in bed? We have. Late one night we were sitting downstairs in our family room. I (*Patrick*) was venting—grumbling about ministry, relationships, our minivan, and just about everything else you can imagine! It was not a conversation I would want replayed.

And then I heard it. One of our children had been at the top of the stairs listening to every word that came out of my mouth, every disgruntled complaint that came out of my heart. I was mortified. Ashamed. Convicted. Not simply because I had been heard, but because of what my words revealed about who I was.

Jesus reminds us of a very important truth about our words: they reveal the content of our hearts.

No good tree bears bad fruit, nor does a bad tree bear good fruit. Each tree is recognized by its own fruit. People do not pick figs from thornbushes, or grapes from briers. A good man brings good things out of the good stored up in his heart, and an evil man brings evil things out of the evil stored up in his heart. For the mouth speaks what the heart is full of. (Luke 6:43–45)

Sometimes we may struggle in our communication with our spouse because we are really struggling with the selfish motivations and desires of our own heart. Our words are witnesses, revealing to our spouse (and whoever else may be listening) what we truly desire. And sometimes we want to keep those desires hidden. So what kind of communication are we willing to risk with our spouse? If we suspect that our heart is in the wrong place and talking would just be hurtful to our spouse, we need to turn to Jesus and ask him to fill our heart with his goodness and his grace. Remember, some things are better left unsaid. But we might need to go beyond the "good" and share "the bad and the ugly" as we humbly seek support and accountability from our spouse.

Recently Ruth and the kids were watching a popular cooking show. I was ready for some peace and quiet—alone time was on my agenda! "Why don't you just sit down and join us?" Ruth asked. Instead of communicating wisely, I opted for pacing back and forth from the kitchen, dropping hints with my words and actions that it was bedtime. It wasn't so much what I said, it was how I said it. Once again, my words gave me away! I'm not sure why it's so hard to admit to your spouse when you are struggling. It would have been far better for me to confess my own sin of selfishness.

Without healthy and honest communication, we can never live out God's purpose and plan for our marriage and family. Staying on the same page as a couple when you have kids in the house requires talking often and talking openly. We have to resist the temptation toward selfishness and work together if we are going to keep our love alive when kids come along.

Just the *Two* of Us

In his booklet *Conflict*, Timothy Lane outlines the most common desires that can turn into self-centered demands. Take a moment to talk about which desires best describe your heart.

- **Comfort.** I want, must have, and deserve some rest and relaxation, and you'd better not hinder my ability to get it!
- **Approval.** I want, must have, and deserve your approval, and you'd better give it to me!
- **Success.** I want, must have, and deserve to be successful, and I'll do anything to achieve it.
- **Power.** I want, must have, and deserve power, and I will do anything to have it.[4]

---

4. Timothy Lane, *Conflict* (Greensboro, NC: New Growth Press, 2006), 5–6.

Carve Out Time—Just for Two

We love being parents. There are few things in life that bring as much joy as watching our kids grow up. But we also love quiet time together. It's not uncommon for us to awaken much earlier than our kids do. When that happens, we quickly turn off the alarm and sneak downstairs.

Our early-morning escapes are filled with coffee and quiet conversation—a bit of a retreat during this busy time of our lives. Inevitably that time alone passes by too quickly. Before long, we hear the sound of feet hitting the wood floor above us. When we hear footsteps coming down the stairs, we know it is time to transition our day from couple to family, from time alone to time together. Soon a toddler's or teenager's face will peek around the corner. We put on our mom and dad hats as the day officially kicks into motion.

Every couple with children needs to make time to be alone to talk. It's not that we don't or can't talk throughout the day. There is just a lot less stress and chaos when we are alone trying to communicate. Most of our best communication happens when we are fully engaged with each other and not having to meet the needs of our children. It takes extra effort and a bit of planning to take advantage of the brief moments. It might be sneaking away on a walk, a weekly date night, sitting out on the porch after the kids are in bed, or meeting for lunch during the week.

Whenever and however, this time is needed, isn't it? Communication changes when we have a family, but it doesn't have to cease. We need to make the opportunity to share what is on our hearts. We need to make time to think and talk with each other about the future. And we need together time to sync schedules, check appointments, discuss rides, plan for the week, and coordinate the everyday details of life.

Turning Down the "Heat"

It is no secret that parenting can put a couple on edge. Communication can morph into conflict in an instant. It's not just what we say, but how we say it, that matters. Many conflicts in our home have started due to the way one of us said something.

Fortunately, the New Testament is full of instruction on how to interact with each other. Although an entire book could be written on the fruits of the Spirit (Galatians 5:22–23), we want to highlight just two—kindness and gentleness—that are crucial in communication.

Kindness and gentleness are an expression, or outworking, of love. They have a way of changing the communication climate from war to peace. When we move toward love with each other, we must do so with kindness and gentleness. In his book *The Practice of Godliness*, Jerry Bridges offers helpful insight into these two character qualities.

"Kindness," he says, is the "sincere desire for the happiness of others." It is "our awareness of those around us and the thoughtfulness that we can express to them."[5]

Kindness for a couple may look like smiling at each other, expressing appreciation, encouragement, or recognizing when our spouse has done something good or pleasing.

"Gentleness," on the other hand, is "actively seeking to make others feel at ease, or 'restful,' in our presence."[6] Gentleness de-escalates any tension in a relationship, enabling a husband and wife to feel comfortable communicating. Gentleness helps a couple to talk openly and honestly, without attacking or being defensive.

One of the best illustrations of kindness and gentleness in action is found in a description of Jesus' life and ministry:

---

5. Jerry Bridges, *The Practice of Godliness: Godliness Has Value for All Things* (Colorado Springs: NavPress, 2008), 193.
6. Ibid., 187.

A bruised reed he will not break, and a smoldering wick he will not snuff out, till he has brought justice through to victory. In his name the nations will put their hope. (Matthew 12:20–21)

The language of a "bruised reed" and a "smoldering wick" are generally understood to refer to people. Jesus would not be critical, harsh, overbearing, rude, forceful, or demanding. He would be kind and gentle to people—careful to bend, but never break them. If we are to please God and honor each other with our communication, we must choose our words wisely and speak carefully so that we interact with kindness and gentleness.

Hit the "Pause" Button

"I want everyone to be quiet for five minutes," Ruth announced. "Your dad and I are trying to talk." I looked in the rearview mirror to gauge how effective this was going to be.

One child, who had previously had the window down "mooing" at cows, paused.

Another child, singing loudly while listening to songs on her iPod, stopped.

The other two looked perplexed.

"We are trying to have a serious conversation, and we need a little peace and quiet. Five minutes. No talking," Ruth finished. She said it with such calm and seriousness, for a moment I thought it might actually work. It did—almost. Our peace and quiet lasted closer to two minutes than five. It wasn't nearly enough time for us to finish talking. In hindsight, it was not the best time for us to try to have a serious conversation.

Let's Talk about Disagreements

In Romans 12:18, the apostle Paul writes, "If it is possible, as far as it depends on you, live at peace with everyone." Every couple deals with conflict. Disagreements are inevitable, even in the healthiest marriages. The following list of ways to deal with disagreements can help you communicate in a more God-honoring way as you strive to "live at peace" with one another.

1. Be quick to admit (confess) your own contribution to the conflict. Lead with "I" instead of "you."

2. Be willing to forgive. Guard against living in the past, and don't hold previous wrongs over your spouse's head (Matthew 6:14–15; Ephesians 4:32).

3. Focus not only on what needs to be said, but the best way to say it (Ephesians 4:29).

4. Seek to resolve disagreements sooner rather than later (Matthew 5:23–24).

5. Avoid extremes or exaggerations: "You always . . ."; "Every time . . ."; "I never . . ."

6. Don't respond emotionally—take time to listen and cool off before engaging in conflict (James 1:19–21).

7. Be willing to overlook minor offenses (Proverbs 12:16; 19:11).

8. Don't avoid necessary conflict—stuffing your feelings can lead to bitterness, resentment, and further hurt.

9. Be specific—don't expect your spouse to read your mind.

10. Ask questions—be careful of assumptions or drawing premature conclusions.

11. Try to focus more on the positive instead of the negative (Philippians 2:1–4; 4:8).

As a couple, take some time to discuss which of these is most challenging for you and why. When are the two of you most likely to have unhealthy disagreements? Write down and discuss the top two or three points of conflict most common for you and your family. What can you begin to do differently?

That's the problem for most couples with kids. There is a good time to talk and a million terrible times to talk. Often it is much better to put certain conversations on pause until the kids are in bed and we are alone. This eliminates the added stress, distraction, and noise created by a house (or car) full of kids. Trying to talk about our finances, a crazy schedule, our romantic expectations being disappointed, or a dispute about discipline while kids are running around is like pouring a can of gasoline on a fire.

Cities in the ancient world were often built with walls around them for safety and protection. This is why Proverbs 25:28 says, "Like a city whose walls are broken through is a person who lacks self-control." A couple without self-control is like a city that is weak, vulnerable, and easily defeated. A couple with self-control can prevent disaster or destruction. As parents, it is our responsibility to control what is said, how it is said, and when it is said so that we build safety and security into our marriage and family relationships.

Perhaps one of the most important types of communication to put on pause is conflict. Kids will feel what they can't comprehend. So while it can be helpful for our kids to see how we work together and communicate in a healthy way to solve problems, it is best to have more serious or difficult conversations in their absence. Being careful how we communicate is helpful for creating and maintaining a peaceful and secure environment for our kids. We have a far better chance of communicating the right way when we exercise self-control in the moment by putting some conversations on hold.

Communication: The Skill We All Need for Success

A recent study polled adults on what they thought was the most important skill for kids to possess to succeed in life, and 90 percent identified the ability to communicate.[7] People valued the good old-fashioned kind of communication—face-to-face, talking, listening, understanding, and engaging.

Kids are not the only ones who need to learn to communicate to succeed. Learning to communicate is a lifelong journey, one that is absolutely necessary if we are to live out God's purpose and plan for keeping our vow to love our spouse with kids in the house. Fulfilling this vow won't just happen. It will take grace, intentional effort, and lots of communication for our love to continue to grow deeper and stronger.

---

7. Sara Kehaulani Goo, "The Skills Americans Say Kids Need to Succeed in Life," *Pew Research Center* (February 19, 2015), http://www.pewresearch.org/fact-tank/2015/02/19/skills-for-success/.

— 11 —

TAKING THE FIGHT OUT OF FINANCES

There are two ways to have enough money: one is to acquire more; the other is to desire less.

G. K. Chesterton

I must have been twelve or thirteen when my grandfather caught me looking at a motorcycle catalog I had picked up at the local bike shop in his hometown of Prestonsburg, Kentucky. He was not impressed with my love for motorcycles. "If you want to fly, get your pilot's license," he said.

Legend has it my grandfather had bought a Harley shortly after World War II. Laying it down on a gravel road nearly cost him his life. So one can appreciate his lack of enthusiasm for my interest in riding one someday. But I never grew out of my dream of owning my own bike.

When I was in eighth grade, my dad bought me a moped. By God's grace I survived a few near misses, like the light post in our front yard. Shortly after high school I bought my first motorcycle, a Honda Rebel 250.

During the summer of 2002, a few years after we were married, I had saved enough money to buy the bike of my dreams—a black Harley-Davidson Softail Heritage Classic. It was a beautiful bike. A far cry from my moped! Loaded with chrome, leather saddlebags, more chrome, and a windshield that kept the bugs out of my face, this was a man's bike. I had arrived!

As fast as my dream was realized, it began to unravel. It wasn't an accident that cost me my bike; it was the transition into parenthood. The summer of 2002 also brought our first child into our lives. We became a family, and our finances would never be the same!

While Patrick may have had visions of me on the back of the motorcycle, I (*Ruth*) was having a different kind of vision. I had added up the cost of diapers, baby clothes, medical bills, and strollers, so I was envisioning a "back to reality" kind of talk with him about family and finances. Fortunately he came to his senses before we had "the talk." I was relieved and grateful that, while it wasn't easy for him, he understood that a family brought with it a new set of priorities.

Having a family usually means a new strain on finances, and it's one that doesn't go away. A *New York Times* article notes, "According to the Department of Agriculture, the average middle-class couple will spend $241,080 to raise a child to age 18. Factor in four years of college and maybe graduate school, or a parentally subsidized internship with the local theater company, and say hello to your million-dollar bundle of oh joy."[1]

---

1. Natalie Angier, "The Changing American Family," *New York Times* (November 25, 2013), http://www.nytimes.com/2013/11/26/health/families.html?_r=0.

We get it! Our firstborn, Tyler, is no longer a baby. He just transitioned into adult-sized shoes. The cost of new shoes and clothing alone is enough to give us heart palpitations! Add dental care, sports costs, and groceries, and it is no wonder most couples with kids feel the strain of a tight budget. The cost of children is real, and sometimes there is a lot of "fight" when a couple deals with the financial realities of life with kids in the house.

When resources that are limited to begin with have to stretch to meet even greater needs, a couple can feel a lot of stress. For some couples, the financial stress of becoming a family might mean:

- anxiety over a child's future and well-being;
- going out on fewer (and cheaper) dates;
- opting out of vacation time;
- an inability to save for emergencies and future needs;
- saying good-bye to discretionary funds for nicer clothing, home furnishings, or hobbies.

Over time, the new financial dynamics can take a toll on a marriage. As much as kids are a blessing, the pressure to provide for them can be a heavy weight for many couples. The result can be conflict, discouragement, and even distance between husband and wife.

Kids + Money = Stress

A recent *Money* magazine article about money and couples highlights what most couples, especially those with kids, already know: married couples fight a lot about finances. According to the statistics, "70 percent of married couples argue about money—ahead of fights about household chores, togetherness, sex, snoring, and what's for dinner."[2]

What we found interesting is that couples whose kids were over age eighteen experienced less conflict over finances than couples with children who were younger than eighteen. The article reports that 80 percent of couples with children younger than eighteen argue over money, while 64 percent of couples with children over eighteen indicate money as a source of conflict. For most couples, having kids in the house throws gasoline on the financial fires.

A February 2015 CNN report notes that "people living in lower-income households, parents of children under 18, Millennials and Gen Xers were among the most likely to report high levels of money stress."[3]

The biggest reason couples fight over finances is because of spending. According to the research, 55 percent of fighting over finances relates to spending, while only 37 percent relates to saving. When you add the needs of kids to the mix, it is easy to see that unexpected costs, medical bills, sports, extracurricular activities, clothing, student loans, and electronic devices only heighten what is already a touchy subject in most marriages.

Managing our spending was, and can still be, a great source of conflict for us. Raising kids raises expenses, so the resources we have must accomplish more. This was quite an adjustment for us, as it is for many couples. Some of our needs,

2. Cybele Weiser, "Richer, Together," *Money* (June 2014): 58–65.
3. Melanie Hicken, "Money Issues Are Still Stressing Americans Out," *CNN Money* (February 4, 2015), http://money.cnn.com/2015/02/04/pf/money-stress/.

and most of the time our wants, had to take a backseat to our children's needs. Any couple that doesn't have a selfless attitude in this area is certain to experience conflict.

We can't escape the reality that finances, and how unified we are in managing them, play a significant role in how healthy our marriage is. To keep our love alive when kids come along, it becomes more important than ever to take the fight out of our finances.

Spender + Saver + Conflict = Disaster

When we first married, we lived in a basement apartment in Lincoln Park, Chicago, while we completed our final year at Moody. We had an antique wooden desk in our tiny kitchen where we kept all of the bills and other financial papers. During those early years, I (*Patrick*) kept track of our finances. I scribbled our weekly and monthly expenses plus our meager income on a piece of paper. I had charts illustrating what we needed and what we had. It wasn't a sophisticated system, but at least we had a plan. It lasted about two months.

The problem was, we had opposing views about money. In fact, our views of money and finances couldn't have been more different when we first got married. One was a saver, the other a spender. Neither of us was terribly skilled in financial management, let alone conflict resolution. We knew marriage had its own stresses, but we never guessed finances would be one of our biggest. The combination proved dangerous.

During the first few years of our marriage, we made about every financial mistake a young couple could make. We leased a car, bought a house, financed new furniture, took in a dog, then a second dog, and finally, bought the Harley. Before the days of Dave Ramsey, I (*Patrick*) had listened to almost every financial broadcast by Larry Burkett. Unfortunately, marriage undid everything I had learned. With every unwise financial decision we made, I not only felt uncomfortable, I could heard Larry "whispering" in my ear!

One of our poor decisions would have been bad enough, but the culmination of them with the addition of our first child had us in a hole that took us years to get out of. The differences we had over dollars brought its share of division into our marriage, and we often wish we could have a do-over of those early years.

Fortunately, we're not left to figure it all out on our own. God's reign and rule in our lives extends to our finances, and Jesus was not shy when it came to talking about money. It's impossible to separate faith, finances, and family. Throughout the Bible we are encouraged to have a life perspective that keeps our financial priorities in the right order. The life and financial priorities outlined in the Bible include the following:

- Work hard (Proverbs 6:6–8; 10:4; Colossians 3:23; 1 Timothy 5:8).
- Save wisely (Proverbs 21:20).
- Avoid debt (Psalm 37:21; Proverbs 22:7).
- Give generously (Proverbs 22:9; 2 Corinthians 9:7; 1 Timothy 6:17–19).
- Flee from the love of money (Proverbs 28:22; Luke 12:15; 1 Timothy 6:6–8).
- Find our real security and hope in God (Hebrews 13:5–6; 1 Timothy 6:17–19).

In Luke 12, Jesus finds himself in the middle of a family feud. Apparently two brothers were in a dispute over their inheritance. Jesus uses the situation as an opportunity to teach that life is about far more than money. He says to them,

> "Man, who appointed me a judge or an arbiter between you?" Then he said to them, "Watch out! Be on your guard against all kinds of greed; life does not consist in an abundance of possessions." (Luke 12:14–15)

Money isn't everything. "Life does not consist in an abundance of possessions."

Living on less doesn't equal living less. Keeping this perspective about money is critical if we are going to live in financial unity as a couple, especially when we have kids in the house. This was not easy for us to learn. Not only were our finances out of order because of the things we acquired unwisely, but we were shocked by what happened to our stuff once we had kids in the house.

No matter how hard you try to steward your stuff, kids are hard on it. We've had car doors nicked by scooters, couches seasoned with Gatorade, bikes left out in the rain, and shoes left out and eaten by the dog. And we won't even tell you how many times we had to replace the once perfect, but hopelessly stained, pale gray rug Ruth found for our dining room. Just repairing damage sucks money into a giant black hole.

For a long time we struggled with this. The mistake we made was to think that having more meant living more. Somehow we thought that we would be happier, more satisfied if we had more of the things we wanted. Sure, it's nice to have a little extra in savings, it's nice to have some of the things we want and enjoy, and it's nice to eat out more than once a month. But these things don't bring life to living.

Finally we realized that life is about far more than stuff. No amount of money or possessions could compare to the moments we have had to enjoy life with our kids, including:

- staying up late to practice soccer drills;
- relaxing in bed talking and laughing;
- reading one more book to the kids;
- movie night at home;
- pizza and popcorn for dinner.

These are the moments our kids will remember the most. It's our relationship, the moments together—not the money or stuff—that counts.

Just the *Two* of Us

Take some time together to discuss some ways you can work together to take the fight out of your finances. Don't try to solve it all at once. Start with small steps that both of you can support.

- In what ways could we focus on living more even though we may be living with less?

- What changes in our finances would be most beneficial for our marriage during this season of life?

- What adjustments in ordering our financial priorities could make a positive difference in our marriage relationship?

When we started to put our financial life in its proper place, it took much of the fight and stress out of our marriage. We discovered that living on less is not the same as living less. We can live—even live well—on less, but it requires learning to live within our limits.

Learning to Live within Our Limits

One of the best ways to avoid or minimize financial stress is to live wisely within our limits. Disregarding a budget and living with no limits is a sure way to bring on the stress of living in debt. Trust us, we know!

The Bible consistently warns us about the dangers of living beyond what we can afford. Notice the warnings about living without financial limits:

> The rich rule over the poor, and the borrower is slave to the lender. (Proverbs 22:7)

> No one can serve two masters. Either you will hate the one and love the other, or you will be devoted to the one and despise the other. You cannot serve both God and money. (Matthew 6:24)

Debt can become an overwhelming burden. And it isn't just debt that can put a financial strain on a marriage. Sacrificing too much, as in spending beyond what we really have available to spend, enslaves us as well.

For example, we recently talked with a couple about the challenge of travel sports. With four kids in our house, we have wrestled with how much money is okay to spend on travel sports or other higher cost extracurricular activities. The couple we talked with lamented the strain their son's travel league was putting on them. They hadn't taken on financial debt for his activities, but they hadn't vacationed in years because the cost of tournaments had eaten up their ability to get away. This is an easy trap to fall into. The financial stress of keeping kids involved in different sports or activities can be a harsh taskmaster, creating a lot of marital stress.

So how do we live within limits? First, we work on it together. We reaffirm our financial and family priorities so that we can make a plan for the future, so we know when to say yes and when to say no when it comes to financial decisions. Just this one commitment goes a long way toward helping us to live within limits and lessen the stress on our marriage.

The next step is to adjust our spending. Both of us have had to curb our spending since kids came along. Depending on your financial situation, this might mean agreeing to not buy the most expensive clothing, shoes, or household items. It might mean going without "wants" for the sake of needs during this season. It may mean restricting the activities our kids are involved in instead of allowing them to be involved in anything and everything. And for some families facing exceptional financial challenges, it might mean seeking assistance for necessities from family, friends, or their local church.

Deciding to live within our limits requires us to ignore what other families are doing. It means refusing to fall into the trap of comparing or competing. It means making a decision to live wisely with what God has given us and where he has us. While it may be tough, it is well worth what we gain in return.

"Our" Money, Not "My" Money

When we come together in marriage, the Bible tells us we become "one flesh." Our oneness is intended to be about all of life, not just what happens in the bedroom. Learning to work together as one team with our finances is incredibly important. In real life, however, financial oneness often doesn't happen.

Inevitably, when I (*Patrick*) counsel couples, the issue of money comes up. Often I will hear them speak in terms of "my money" versus "your money." One spouse says, "Well, I pay the house payment, cars, and cell phones. What about you?" Or, as one working mom said, "It's my job and my paycheck—you can't tell me what to do with it." These are always awkward, painful moments in counseling, and they are not uncommon.

As long as we are thinking "mine" rather than "ours," countless opportunities for financial conflict will arise. "Mine" means we are not working together. We are operating as two individuals instead of one team. It's helpful to move from thinking and talking in terms of "my money" to thinking and talking of "our money."

When we first married we made the decision to become one, even in our finances. Our attitude is that we don't get to pick and choose which areas we will and won't walk in oneness. So, from the beginning, we attempted to work as one team when it came to finances. When both of us worked outside the home, we didn't focus on how much each of us made individually; we focused on what we earned together.

In our home, we have worked together to establish a budget, working out what is best for our marriage and family during different seasons. We talk often and openly about income, expenses, savings, and current and future needs.

Although our individual abilities mean that I (*Patrick*) do more of the planning and budgeting and Ruth makes sure the bills are paid, we are both involved, working together to manage our finances. Everything we have and own is one because we are one.

Just the *Two* of Us

To take the fight out of finances, we need to work together as one. We need to stop using the word *mine* and start using the word *ours*. Talk about how you and your spouse might start working as one on your finances.

- What might change if you communicated more frequently about your finances?

- How beneficial would it be to establish a budget together?

- What might change if you were more willing to listen to each other and compromise when it comes to financial decisions?

Decide Today What You Will Do for Your Kids Tomorrow

The future will be here before we know it. If you are reading this and your children are young, it's hard to imagine them taking their first driving lesson or going off to college. If your kids are old enough to talk, you're getting a hint of what lies ahead. Chances are they are already asking about electronic devices—tablets, computers, and cell phones. Those milestones are not that far away.

No matter what their ages are today, you already know that the day they leave your house is coming quickly. Just the other day we were discussing how our oldest son will be in college in only four years! So living on purpose and with a plan is critical. Consider the wisdom of thinking and planning ahead that is found in the following Bible passages:

> The plans of the diligent lead to profit as surely as haste leads to poverty. (Proverbs 21:5)

> The wise store up choice food and olive oil, but fools gulp theirs down. (Proverbs 21:20)

> Suppose one of you wants to build a tower. Won't you first sit down and estimate the cost to see if you have enough money to complete it? For if you lay the foundation and are not able to finish it, everyone who sees it will ridicule you, saying, "This person began to build and wasn't able to finish." (Luke 14:28–30)

The principle to be gleaned from each of these passages is that those who are wise begin now to plan and save for later. It is not always easy to work a plan. In our first several years of ministry, we thought, *How in the world can we possibly save for the future when we are barely making it from paycheck to paycheck?* At that time, we couldn't save for the future the way we wanted to, but we could talk about it, we could plan for it, and we could start saving for tomorrow.

One of the growing trends in our culture that every couple

Let's Talk about Finances for Our Family

Below are some questions to help you think through and talk about some of the difficult, but important, decisions you need to make for your family's future financial needs. These conversations will take time, thought, and plenty of grace as you seek as a couple to obey God's Word and to do what is best for your family.

- At what age or according to which criteria will we allow our kids to get a cell phone, and will they be responsible to pay for it?

- Will our kids be responsible for purchasing their own car? What financial assistance, if any, will we offer them?

- Should we try to pay for our children's college? If so, how much will we attempt to save to help them offset the expense?

- How can we begin helping our kids manage their money well?

- What is an appropriate allowance?

- How might we teach our children to save when they receive a gift, allowance, or paycheck?

- What do our spending habits teach our children?

- What do we communicate to our kids verbally and nonverbally about working hard?

- Are we teaching our kids to give? Do we give generously to our local church, and are we encouraging our kids to do the same?

- How can we do a better job teaching and modeling generosity to those who are in need?

- As our kids get older, and clothing gets more expensive, what will we expect them to pay for?

- In how many sporting activities or extracurricular activities should we allow our kids to participate during a year?

with kids has to face is what is being called (among other things) "extended adolescence, youthhood, adultolescence, the twixter years, young adulthood, the twenty-somethings, and emerging adulthood."[4] It is a trend that can place significant pressure on family finances and added stress, even conflict, on a couple's relationship.

Dr. Christian Smith, a sociology professor at Notre Dame University, describes emerging adulthood as "a time of limbo, of transition, of being neither a teen nor a real adult."[5] While he cites various causes of this social trend (higher education, delaying marriage, less secure careers, birth control, and postmodernism), he identifies one that is especially important to parents who are raising kids: financial support of parents. Commenting on this particular cause, he writes:

Parents of today's youth, aware of the resources it often takes to succeed, seem increasingly willing to extend financial and other support to their children well into

---

4. Christian Smith, Kari Christoffersen, Hilary Davidson, and Patricia Snell Herzog, *Lost in Transition: The Dark Side of Emerging Adulthood* (New York: Oxford University Press, 2011), 15.

5. Ibid., 231–32.

their 20s and perhaps early 30s. According to best estimates, American parents spend on their children an average of $33,340 per child in total material assistance (cash, housing, educational expenses, food, etc.) over the 17-year period between ages 18 and 34. These resources help to subsidize emerging adults' freedom to take a good, long time before settling down into full adulthood.[6]

The idea is that the transition into adulthood is taking much longer than it ever has before. Obviously we cannot be certain of all the circumstances that will exist when our kids enter that transition from adolescence to adulthood. But our awareness allows us to begin talking about how we can best prepare our children to succeed when they leave home. It can motivate us to teach our kids the value of money, hard work, praying about what God wants them to do, responsibility, and even saving their own money for the future.

Not one of us knows what tomorrow will bring. By simply learning to plan together for the future today, while trusting God for tomorrow, we can take unnecessary stress and conflict out of our marriage.

Remembering Our Hope and Security

The greatest protection against financial stress and conflict is an abiding assurance in God's faithfulness. God controls the future, so we don't have to. No matter what the season or its unique demands, we are not walking through life alone!

---

6. Ibid., 14.

As we look back over the last seventeen years of marriage, we have experienced plenty of scary times financially. During one such time, I (*Patrick*) took on a second job in addition to my pastoral responsibilities to pay some bills. But as we reflect on those times, we can honestly say, as hard as some of them were, God as a faithful Father always provided what we needed. Yes, we went without wants at times (and sometimes what we thought were needs). We also experienced times when friends paid our bills after we suddenly lost our income. But God has always come through, doing exactly what he said he would do.

In the parable of the rich fool in Luke 12, Jesus teaches that placing too much trust in money is just as dangerous as loving money too much. He used the rich man in the parable as an illustration that greed can be evident in not only having a lot of money and not sharing it but also in placing too much hope in money. The rich man's inability to give to others was motivated by a desire to guard what was his to protect only himself. He was building bigger barns to store his excess in an effort to ensure greater security for himself.

We must realize that greed is not only misplaced treasure; it is misplaced trust. No wonder greed is so offensive to God, our Father, who loves and protects his own. Confidence in the goodness of our Father frees us from unnecessary stress and anxiety. Security is not dependent on how big our barn is, but rather how great our God is. This is precisely why Jesus, in the very next passage, tells us not to worry:

> Then Jesus said to his disciples: "Therefore I tell you, do not worry about your life, what you will eat; or about your body, what you will wear. For life is more

than food, and the body more than clothes. Consider the ravens: They do not sow or reap, they have no storeroom or barn; yet God feeds them. And how much more valuable you are than birds! Who of you by worrying can add a single hour to your life? Since you cannot do this very little thing, why do you worry about the rest?" (Luke 12:22–26)

Financial peace is found in Fatherly dependence, not financial independence. True security is being confident that God is our Father. He has given us great and precious promises that he will supply us with all we need. One of our favorite verses that reminds us of God's presence and power to provide is Hebrews 13:5:

Keep your lives free from the love of money and be content with what you have, because God has said, "Never will I leave you; never will I forsake you."

While marriage with kids in the house stretches our resources thinner and squeezes our budgets tighter, we have a Father who knows our needs. He has given us his Word to guide us, helping us to walk wisely so that finances don't divide what he has joined together during this expensive, but good, season of marriage and family.

A Test of Your Togetherness

When Life Gets Really Hard

*Praise be to the God and Father of our Lord Jesus
Christ, the Father of compassion and the God of
all comfort, who comforts us in all our troubles,
so that we can comfort those in any trouble with
the comfort we ourselves receive from God.*

2 Corinthians 1:3–4

In 2010 my *(Patrick's)* dad passed away suddenly in a car accident, and our world turned upside down. Nobody can prepare you for a phone call like that. When Ruth walked into the house with the kids and looked at me, she could instantly tell something terrible had happened without my saying a word. It was a new kind of suffering for us, the kind we would not get over easily.

My mom lived two hours away from us and was unable to live on her own. She immediately became a concern for my sisters and me. It would cost all of us time, energy, and resources. There was no getting over it, only getting through it. We were all suddenly thrust into a new season of life that included suffering. Our new normal was overwhelming. How would we navigate this tragedy on top of an already busy season? How would it impact our kids? How would we find time for all that needed to be done? How would we find time for each other? The hard stuff, no matter what it is, tests our togetherness.

A husband and father dealing with the loss of a job may feel intense fear, anger, and isolation. The last thing on his mind is how he can nurture his marriage.

A couple who lose a loved one—a parent, a friend, a child—spiral into months or even years of grief. Romance, intimacy, and cultivating the marriage relationship are the last things on their mind when they are just trying to survive one day at a time.

A couple with a special-needs child can feel lonely, frustrated, and resentful of friends and family members who seem to abandon them to enjoy their own lives. Meeting their child's needs demands and deserves nearly every ounce of energy they have, leaving little to share with each other.

A husband and wife whose child has been abused or molested may free-fall into guilt, accusations, or blaming. Why couldn't we (or you) protect our child? What could or should we (or you) have done differently? Their togetherness may unravel.

A couple discouraged by the challenges of a second marriage may think, *It would be easier to go our separate ways. Admit it didn't work. Trying to blend our families is too hard.* They may feel too defeated to nurture what they fear is another failed relationship.

All of these challenging situations and more can crush a marriage. The hard stuff can drive a couple to try to escape the pain and flee from each other in the process.

The hard stuff of life is all around us. It hits close to home in the form of job losses, sickness, death, tragedy, miscarriages, strained finances, abuse, or disabilities. It's found in blended families and traditional families. Bullied children, kids struggling in school, kids with autism, paralysis, or mental illness all take their toll. Everywhere we look, there is evidence that we are not in the garden anymore. God's original creation has been tainted by sin. So suffering, in time, leaves its mark on all of us.

Hope for Our Most Difficult Trials

Even though Jesus told us that trials in life are inevitable (John 16:33), we are still surprised by them, mad at them, and at times, defeated by them. God's intent for intimacy and friendship in marriage can be severely tested when these trials come because the hard stuff has a way of testing our togetherness.

The good news is, God does not abandon us in the tough times. While we may feel helpless, in Jesus we have all the resources we need to live out our marriage vows—together. Trials don't have to tear us apart.

In fact, author Dan Allender writes, sometimes God "takes us into the depths of our despair in order for a new hope to be born."[1] It is possible to come through our trials with a hope

---

1. Dan Allender, *The Healing Path: How the Hurts in Your Past Can Lead You to a More Abundant Life* (Colorado Springs: WaterBrook, 1999), 27.

and joy that is more securely set on the truth and promises of Christ. God can and does use the hard stuff for our good. In marriage, our trials can be a doorway into greater maturity, intimacy, and dependence on God's grace.

So how do we get through the bad stuff? How do we find hope when we're living in the middle of the hard stuff? How do we stick together when we are overwhelmed? There is no one method or formula for dealing with all that life throws at us. And sometimes "getting over" the challenges is impossible. But there are hopeful and God-honoring ways to get through the pain, and they begin by not just getting through them but getting through them together.

I (*Patrick*) wouldn't have been able to put my finger on it at the time. In the midst of the whirlwind after my dad died, I didn't notice what was happening, and I certainly had no time for reflection. I was in over my head. What we were up against was too much for one person to handle. It took all hands on deck just to stay afloat. But at some point after my mom passed away, it occurred to me that Ruth had never once complained during the two years we helped to care for my mom. Wow! I know full well those years weren't easy for her. I spent time away, and she took on additional responsibilities that I usually did, including parenting alone on many occasions. We had extra expenses, and the two of us had less time together. All of it took its toll not only on me but also on us as a couple and as a family. Looking back, it is a miracle we all survived! Things were different and harder, but Ruth never allowed the disruption it brought to our "normal life" to come between us.

As much as those years were a blur, I now see clearly how our marriage stayed strong as we were struggling to get

Commitments That Matter

Biblical love is not about how we feel; it is about how we take action. It is a deep commitment to honor God and honor each other no matter how hard life gets. We have found the following five commitments to be helpful when walking through painful seasons as a couple.

1. **We trust what God's Word says and not just how we feel.** It is so easy to be ruled by our emotions. Even when we don't feel like it, we allow God's truth and promises to be our anchor.

2. **We will pray and read God's Word together regularly.** We will not let our hurt dislodge us from abiding in Christ. We will run to him and not from him during this painful time.

3. **We will be selfless lovers.** We will have a servant attitude and not allow our expectations, desires for comfort, or selfishness to get in the way of honoring Christ and each other.

4. **We will talk often and talk openly.** We will share our hearts with each other, ask questions, and stay connected, especially when it would be easy to withdraw or shut down.

5. **We will not walk through this alone.** We will reach out to friends, family, and our church to help us get through the hard stuff.

through. Ruth was in it with me. We were getting through it together.

We did not live a picture-perfect marriage during those years. There were no consistent date nights. Our romantic moments were far fewer. We were in survival mode, but surviving together.

Hard stuff doesn't allow for a me-centered marriage. The kind of God-honoring marriage and family we said we wanted and were willing to work for when we made our wedding vows requires being selfless lovers. The hard stuff puts that vow to the test. Our actions always reveal what we really believe. We'd made the vow; when the hard stuff hit, it was time to keep the vow. Thankfully, Ruth and I are persevering, not always perfectly, but we're still getting through it together.

Pain Is Part of Our Journey

My (*Ruth's*) hopes were crushed—utterly crushed—and not for the second or even the third time, but for the fifth time.

I cried out to the nurse, "I don't get it! Why does this keep happening?"

All of my blood vials, needle pokes, doctor visits, weigh-ins, and vital signs indicated that this time, at twenty weeks along in my pregnancy, I should be seeing a healthy and strong heartbeat from the child still in my womb. Instead, I stared silently, shocked, in disbelief at my perfectly healthy baby whose heart had stopped beating for no apparent reason.

Why, God? This is the fifth time! Why does this keep happening? Why?

Instantly I began to sink inward. I began to withdraw,

pulling in close all of the disappointment, questions, and anger. I was reeling from the pain of losing another unborn child. I wanted to forget about everything else.

I not only was hurting deeply, I at times felt guilty for what I was feeling or the questions I wrestled with. And life with kids in the house didn't stop. Patrick and I still had jobs to do, a house to take care of, a ministry to run, and kids to raise. It was too much. Instead of engaging, I withdrew. For a time, I even withdrew from Patrick.

I (*Patrick*) realized that the hurt Ruth was experiencing was very different from what I was experiencing. I struggled to understand and feel what she felt. I learned to listen, resisting the temptation to try to fix anything. She didn't need me to push her to get stronger; she needed me to be patient while God brought healing. I did my best to give her space to be alone, permission to not have it all together, and time to let God do what only he could do.

She needed to know that as a mom, who is so used to giving, it was okay to be on the receiving end. Even our kids chipped in! We did our best to do the things Ruth usually does. Our older kids will tell you that they rose to the challenge—keeping their rooms clean, helping with laundry, grabbing Ruth something to eat, or just snuggling on the couch. It was a team effort. Something we were committed to getting through together.

In the Bible, the book of Job tells the story of a man whose family was hit hard. Hard times hit every sphere of his life—his wealth dwindled, his children died, and his health declined. The hurt and spiritual questioning that Job expresses throughout the book is raw. It's the stuff of real life. Job reminds us that it is not only okay to hurt but that there

Just the *Two* of Us

Take time together to talk about how handling the hard stuff together could make your marriage stronger.

- If you are in the middle of hard stuff right now, what do each of you need most from the other?
- What are you learning that you might not have realized without this trial?
- How might God use your experience to encourage other couples who face similar circumstances?

is a right way to hurt. For Job, his hurting was heavenward. Timothy Keller summarizes it nicely when he says about Job:

> Yes, he complained to God. He doubted, but he doubted to God. He screamed and yelled, but he did it in God's presence. No matter how much in agony he was, he continued to address God. He kept seeking him. And in the end, God said Job triumphed.[2]

Job's hard stuff drew him in closer to the throne of God's grace, showing that our doubts and struggles can lead to greater devotion. It is not easy to stand together as a couple, or with a spouse, when you are dealing with pain at such a deep level. Job's wife didn't exactly stand with him. In fact, she said to him, "Are you still maintaining your integrity? Curse

---

2. Timothy Keller, *Walking with God through Pain and Suffering* (New York: Dutton, 2013), 287.

God and die!" (Job 2:9). Pain has a way of either leading to distance or to greater devotion to God and to each other. The hard stuff can be an opportunity for us to see that it is our privilege and a precious gift from God when we continue to love and walk through such times together.

Being Patient with God, and with Each Other

We hate to wait for anything. When our microwave conked out on us, you would have thought our kids were going to starve to death! Ten minutes to warm up a bowl of soup or piece of pizza, compared to thirty seconds, felt like an eternity. Just this past week I overheard Ruth mumbling with frustration at her computer because a page wasn't loading fast enough. To be fair, I do the same. The irony is the faster and more convenient things have become, the more impatient we have become.

When it comes to being patient, we certainly don't like to be patient with God or one another when we suffer. Yet patience is what is most required, especially during times of suffering, as James reminds us:

> Be patient, then, brothers and sisters, until the Lord's coming. See how the farmer waits for the land to yield its valuable crop, patiently waiting for the autumn and spring rains. You too, be patient and stand firm, because the Lord's coming is near. . . . As an example of patience in the face of suffering, take the prophets who spoke in the name of the Lord. As you know, we count as blessed

those who have persevered. You have heard of Job's perseverance and have seen what the Lord finally brought
about. The Lord is full of compassion and mercy. (James
5:7–8, 10–11)

These verses remind us that there is much to be gained by
being patient in our suffering, by persevering during the hard
times. Be patient because the Lord is coming. This season
will not have the final say. Be patient because God is at work.
Waiting is not wasted time. Be patient because God is with
you, full of compassion and mercy to comfort you. You can't
hurry through the hurt, so be patient in the pain. The hard
stuff is not to be rushed. We can be patient in the pain because
of the hope we have in Christ. We can be patient in the middle
of the hurt, knowing that we will eventually be blessed, if not
in this life, then in the life to come.

As a couple, we need to be patient in waiting on God when
we endure life's difficult and painful times. We also need to be
patient with each other. As we work to get through the hard
stuff together, we need to remember that what we face can hit
each of us differently. We might not deal with the hard stuff in
the same way or on the same timeline. A husband might take
it in and internalize it. A wife might verbalize her pain, gradu-
ally healing as she talks about it. A couple usually experience
vastly different emotions: one spouse might be depressed; the
other, angry or resentful. The process of dealing with hurt and
grief is not predictable. The pain, questions, and insecurities
come and go at different times.

All of these ups and downs are okay, if not necessary, to
healing. We truly are God's gift to our spouse when we give
each other permission to hurt and patience while we hurt.

No matter where we are in the process of dealing with the hard things in life—a miscarriage, financial setback, disability, injury, death—we need to stay open with each other. We need to be with each other. It's a major part of getting through the hurt together.

- We need to talk.
- We need to ask questions.
- We need to listen carefully to our spouse's response.
- We need to admit when we can't go on.
- We need to vent our frustrations.

Because we grieve in different ways and at different times, we have to keep our hearts open to each other. We need to love and walk with our spouse no matter what. God is using our suffering to change us, giving us the opportunity to draw on one another's strengths when suffering hits. He is filling up what is lacking in us:

Consider it pure joy, my brothers and sisters, whenever you face trials of many kinds, because you know that the testing of your faith produces perseverance. Let perseverance finish its work so that you may be mature and complete, not lacking anything. (James 1:2–4)

When we suffer, God accomplishes his work in different degrees and at different times. Being patient with each other means not trying to fix where our spouse happens to be on the journey. It's leaving room for God to do the work when and how he wants to. Being patient extends extra grace, understanding that this too is a part of God's transforming work in our lives.

During the hard stuff, our faith gets tested and refined. We discover what our faith is really made of. As we walk through the process, we need to have patience with God and with each other. And yet, as valuable as we are to each other, sometimes we need more than our love for each other to get through.

We Need the Church

I (*Patrick*) grew up as a pastor's kid. Church is what we did Sunday morning, Sunday night, Wednesday night, and sometimes more. I grew up seeing the good, bad, and ugly that comes along with being a part of the "already" but "not yet" family of God. I (*Ruth*) didn't become a Christian until later in life. I was drawn to the church not just because the programs and events were fun but because there was something wonderful about the way people looked after one another. For me, the church was a beautiful community of people who deeply and genuinely cared for each other and the world.

We love the church. We need it. Community is central to what it means to be a Christian, and the church is where we find that community. We love how Tim Chester and Steve Timmis describe the beauty of being the church:

> Jesus came to create a people who would model what it means to live under his rule. It would be a glorious outpost of the kingdom of God, an embassy of heaven. This is where the world can see what it means to be truly human.[3]

---

3. Tim Chester and Steve Timmis, *Total Church: A Radical Reshaping around Gospel and Community* (Wheaton: Crossway, 2008), 50.

The New Testament gives many commands that are meant to bind us together in a family larger than our biological family. We are to love each other (John 15:12), carry each other's burdens (Galatians 6:2), be devoted to one another (Romans 12:10), build others up (Ephesians 4:29), accept one another (Romans 15:7), humbly serve one another (Galatians 5:13), encourage one another (1 Thessalonians 5:11), forgive each other (Ephesians 4:32), and pray for each other (James 5:16).

These verses remind us that Jesus redefines family. He expands the circle. He creates a new family joined together in him.

What does this have to do with loving our spouse in the hard stuff of life? Sometimes as a couple the hard stuff is bigger than we are. We need help. We need our extended church family to go through it with us.

Nearly twenty years ago, a couple who have been like spiritual parents to us experienced a life-altering tragedy. Their son's life, and theirs, changed instantly when a car accident permanently confined their son to a wheelchair. For more than 150 days, the mother never left her son's bedside. The couple grieved, pulled together, juggled responsibilities, and began the long journey of getting through it.

When they finally brought their son home from the hospital, they drove down their street and saw their church family lined along both sides of the street. For months, their church family had prayed for them, wept with them, brought them meals, and sent them cards. Now they welcomed them home. They stood, lining the street, not only to be seen but as a symbolic way of saying, We are standing for you and with you. You are not going to walk through this hard stuff alone. We are going to get through this together!

When the hard stuff hits, we need each other—our spouse and our extended church family. The church can and should be a refuge, a people and place of hope in the middle of hurt. This is exactly what the church is called to do with and for one another. When it does, it is beautiful.

Finding Hope in How God's Story Ends

I (*Ruth*) have shared the story of my miscarriages many times. One time, after sharing it at a conference, a woman approached me about how my story ended. Excited, she asked, "So you never shared the rest of the story. What happened after that last miscarriage?"

My reply? "That's it. That *is* the story."

I am sure this well-meaning mom hoped to hear that I had finally given birth to a healthy baby after that last miscarriage. She wanted the "and they lived happily ever after" fairy-tale resolution.

But sometimes a story is just what it is. A heartache happens. Hard stuff doesn't get easier. Years pass. Grief settles in. Memories repeat and replay.

Not every tragic story or disappointment ends with a great reversal. Our stories in this life will not always end happily. While God did bless me with four children who are alive and well, I will never ever be the same after walking through the anguish of losing five babies.

We don't always get an explanation for our suffering. What God does give us is the blessing of walking with one another through the hard stuff. Encouraging one another, praying for one another, crying with one another, and reminding one another of God's character regardless of the circumstances.

Life is hard. Not a day goes by that I don't think of my babies gone from here but waiting for me in heaven. But I know that in God's economy no tear is wasted, no pain is unseen, no heartache goes unnoticed, no agony is unobserved. God is working in and through the trials.

When we are tempted to get angry, bitter, or resentful, we need to remember whose story we are really living in. By God's grace, we need to come back to the main Character. All things, even the hard stuff, God is using as a part of his story.

Life is not always easy, but surrendering the outcomes and expectations to what God is doing, and will do, is critical. Living out the missing vow involves remembering that our marriage has a mission. Our relationship is a part of something bigger than just our romance. Even in loss, unexpected events, tragedies, and suffering, we are witnesses to who God is.

The hard stuff can drive us into a deeper relationship with each other. The hurt is still there, but the hurt is less when we have our togetherness. Looking beyond the pain, we can walk with Jesus through afflictions and into the arms of the Father, all the while trusting that God is doing something with our hard stuff. We may not always understand it, but we have a promise that God is using the hurt in his story. It is this confidence that enables a marriage and family to persevere in the middle of our fallen and hard stories. Our pain comes with a promise—it is not being wasted, and one day he will do away with the hard stuff, once and for all.

— 13 —

YOU WILL LIVE THROUGH THIS!

It is what Jesus is, not what we are, that gives
rest to the soul.
    Charles Spurgeon, *Morning and Evening*

Our kids are growing up fast. We finally traded in our minivan for an SUV. We no longer find scattered Cheerios, old pacifiers, worn board books, and fermented sippy cups. Instead we find soccer cleats, sweaty socks, Gatorade bottles, phone chargers, math books, and iPods.

Recently, we spent a Friday night looking through old scrapbooks—a blue one, a pink one, a red one, and digital photos that will eventually make their way into a scrapbook (maybe). During those early years, I (*Ruth*) zealously snapped photos of our children and carefully crafted the memories in scrapbooks. As the years wear on, fewer pictures make the transition from my phone to a scrapbook.

As we looked through those scrapbooks that night as a family, I just couldn't believe how much the kids have changed and how much we have changed. We found pictures from so many different ages and stages:

- hospital photos
- first steps
- riding bikes
- baby dedications
- soccer games
- baseball games
- setting up Christmas trees
- vacation trips to Tennessee, Colorado, Florida, and Virginia
- parents, grandparents, aunts, uncles, cousins
- weddings and funerals
- Patrick even found pictures of himself with hair!

As photos always do, they took us back to different seasons of life. Some were really good and some really hard. When life comes at you fast, you don't always realize how far you've traveled until you look back. It was a good reminder of not only what we've been through but also how we got through (sometimes just barely).

"Do you remember our first youth ministry trip? The one when we each drove a van loaded with students to Chicago?" Patrick asked.

"How about the summer you were hugely pregnant with Bella and you slept in the closet with Harley [the dog] because she was about to have her puppies?"

"Oh, my goodness, look at how little Tyler and Bella were in that picture!"

We talked about discovering Noah's food allergies the hard and scary way. We reflected on the four-year span when Patrick lost both of his parents and the November when my mom had emergency heart surgery. We remembered how hard it was to sell the home we had lived in for ten years, the home we had brought each of our kids into after they were born.

And we remembered the good times. We talked about how much Bella has grown from being a rule pusher to a young girl who loves to serve and give, often going along on hospital visitations to deliver cards she made. We laughed about Noah's numerous "fashion statements." His flat-bill hats, love for shoes, and long-underwear-under-his-shorts look! We watched videos of Sophia "showcasing" her imagination and creativity. She would often preach sermons to her dolls, dance for us after dinner, and entertain us with humorous stories. And we discussed how Tyler has always been a little man in a child's body—Mr. Responsible. We've always had to remind him he is one of the kids and not a parent!

We didn't always know the road ahead, make the right decision, or have the perfect answers. The anchor that enabled us to stabilize our marriage and family through the various seasons and circumstances was staying close to Jesus. As we sought Jesus first, he faithfully followed through on his promise to take care of everything else (Matthew 6:33).

You Are Following a Person, Not a Formula

Living out God's vision for marriage and family would be a lot easier if there was a formula to follow. We have explored biblical principles and ideas throughout this book, but they are not formulas. There is no A + B = C for living out God's vision for marriage and family. We don't get a foolproof formula, but we do get the invitation to follow Jesus—who, in person, is "the way and the truth and the life" (John 14:6).

I (*Patrick*) was sorting through some books in my office not too long ago when I came across one of my old journals. Like a lot of people, I have kept journals on and off for years. As I skimmed through the pages, I found a thought I had written as a sophomore in college:

> *I try to take each day as a step closer to walking in the right direction. I guess I'm not always sure which way to step. All I can do is be faithful daily and trust that in God's sovereignty, my life will be revealed according to what his will is for me.*

I wrote those words in August 1997, just a year before Ruth and I married. Who knew that just a few months later, a prank phone call would lead to marriage? At the time, I doubt I fully understood how truthful and accurate the words I scribbled in my journal would prove to be.

My first few years in college were confusing, to say the least. Lacking clarity and security, I felt the only thing I knew to do was to stay close to Jesus. If he really was "the way," then it made sense to do my best to keep in step. Jesus didn't say follow the map. He said, "Follow me."

Almost twenty years later, Ruth and I are still trying to keep up with him. As we have matured from college sweethearts, to struggling newlyweds, to excited parents, overwhelmed parents, and beyond, we are still doing our best to stay close to Jesus.

When kids come along, it's easy to get distracted. We hit the ground running each morning. Time is precious and alone time is almost nonexistent. Walking with Jesus and abiding in him requires carving out time and space to be alone with him. This isn't always easy to do, but if we want to keep our marriage and family vibrant, we have to keep our first love alive.

In John 15:1–8, Jesus uses the imagery of a vine and branches to describe what a fruitful and healthy relationship with him looks like:

> I am the true vine, and my Father is the gardener. He cuts off every branch in me that bears no fruit, while every branch that does bear fruit he prunes so that it will be even more fruitful. You are already clean because of the word I have spoken to you. Remain in me, as I also remain in you. No branch can bear fruit by itself; it must remain in the vine. Neither can you bear fruit unless you remain in me.
>
> I am the vine; you are the branches. If you remain in me and I in you, you will bear much fruit; apart from me you can do nothing. If you do not remain in me, you are like a branch that is thrown away and withers; such branches are picked up, thrown into the fire and burned. If you remain in me and my words remain in you, ask whatever you wish, and it will be done for you. This is to my Father's glory, that you bear much fruit, showing yourselves to be my disciples.

On our own, we are lifeless, powerless, and fruitless. We have to walk closely and abide deeply if we want to flourish. We can't love our spouse as God intends unless we stay close to Jesus.

Walking by Faith, Not by Fear

Being a parent is both incredibly fun and incredibly scary. We're not the kind of parents who make our children wear bike helmets in the house or walk with a leash at the supermarket, but we're close. Because our kids are precious to us, we often worry about sickness, tragedy, bullies, financing college, future husbands, future wives, driver's licenses, good grades, bad guys, the Internet, and the orthodontist. These things are enough to send any parent over the edge!

Sometimes we can drive ourselves crazy thinking about the things that could be or might be. Fear can squeeze the joy God intended right out of our marriage and family. J. C. Ryle was right: "Half our miseries are caused by imagining things that we think are coming upon us."[1] If you are anything like we are, then you know it is easy to lie awake at night wondering:

- What if one of our children gets sick?
- What if we can't save enough for college?
- What if one of our sons or daughters walks away from Jesus?
- What if our children get exposed to something we try so hard to protect them from?

This kind of fear or worry does not reveal a heart that trusts God. It reveals a heart that is hopelessly trying to *be* God. Much of our fear and worry is birthed by a prediction of the future where God is not present, active, faithful, good, or

1. J. C. Ryle, *Matthew*, Expository Thoughts on the Gospels (New York: R. Carter, 1860; repr., Carlisle, PA: Banner of Truth Trust, 2012), Kindle edition, section 6:25–34.

powerful enough. Our fears and worries are not just feelings; they can also be an expression of our faith (or lack thereof).

Dan Allender and Tremper Longman write in *Cry of the Soul* that fear asks the question, "Can I trust God to protect me from harm?"[2] Much of our fear predicts that God will not protect, sustain, or guide. In contrast, one of our favorite promises from God is found in Isaiah:

> When you pass through the waters,
>   I will be with you;
> and when you pass through the rivers,
>   they will not sweep over you.
> When you walk through the fire,
>   you will not be burned;
>   the flames will not set you ablaze.
> For I am the LORD your God,
>   the Holy One of Israel, your Savior. . . .
> Do not be afraid, for I am with you.
>   (Isaiah 43:2–3, 5)

While God does not promise us a future without pain, he does promise a future with his presence. We might get wet when we walk through deep waters, but we will not drown. The flames might get hot, but they will not consume us. He will be with us, and it will be enough.

If it weren't for our confidence in God's character, actions, and promises, life would be a lot scarier. Through Jesus, God has given us the hope and assurance that he will never leave us or forsake us. The future is his.

---

2. Dan Allender and Tremper Longman III, *Cry of the Soul: How Our Emotions Reveal Our Deepest Questions about God* (Colorado Springs: NavPress, 1999), 47.

Just the *Two* of Us

Take some time together to talk about how trusting and abiding in Christ can strengthen your marriage.

- How would walking by faith and not by fear make a difference in your relationship?
- In what area or concern is it most difficult for you to "abide in Christ" right now?
- Where do you most need the reminder that "you are going to live through this"?

It is easy to let stress create conflict in marriage. All of the unknowns and real demands of life can drive a couple further apart instead of closer together. So pursuing Christ means we need to seek him, take him at his word, and ultimately let him be God, trusting that he will provide all we need. Proverbs 3:5–6 says it this way:

> Trust in the LORD with all your heart
>   and lean not on your own understanding;
> in all your ways submit to him,
>   and he will make your paths straight.

While much of the future is left undefined, unknown, out of sight, and certainly beyond our power, we can rest in the knowledge that God is a wiser, better, and more powerful parent and provider than we are. What God asks us, and our children, to give him is faithfulness. God wants us to be faithful to him today and trust him for tomorrow. There is joy in letting God be God!

You Will Live through This

"What in the world were we thinking?" I asked Ruth as I laid down yet another puppy pad on our wood floor. We were the proud new owners of Blue, a Labrador puppy affectionately named after our love for Michigan football. We were determined to keep our floors clean during the potty-training phase, which even with close to a dozen puppy pads proved to be unrealistic and impossible. If there was exposed hardwood, Blue found it.

The challenge of life with a new puppy started one night when we were getting ready to go for a family walk after dinner. We already had a dog, Cherry. Cherry is a Pomeranian Maltese and weighs in at about seven pounds. For a dog she is very sophisticated, perhaps even a bit snooty. She doesn't fetch, play with dog toys, or get along with others well. I (*Patrick*) love Cherry, but she's a little embarrassing to walk around the neighborhood. I wanted a man's dog—the kind of dog that runs through rivers, plays fetch, and brings home an occasional kill. The kind of dog you would see on the cover of a fishing or hiking magazine. So I declared to the whole family one night, "I want a man's dog!"

Before long, Ruth found a nearby breeder with new pups. I wanted a dog, but I wasn't sold on the timeline. With four kids, one dog, a hamster, and two books to write, I thought maybe another dog could wait. But Ruth had other plans. And once the kids saw pictures, our decision was made. We were buying a dog.

Two months into puppy training, in frustration I blurted out, "What were we thinking? We already have one dog, a fish, a hamster, four kids, and we are trying to write two books!"

I wasn't finished.

"Our house is a zoo! We have puppy pads everywhere. We are spending a fortune on disinfectant spray and paper towels. We're supposed to be writing in a bookstore or café, not a kennel!"

Ruth, with the patience and precision of Jesus himself, simply looked at me and said, "You are going to live."

Sometimes in the craziness of life, raising kids, managing our home, and trying to keep our love alive, we just need to be reminded, "It's going to be okay. You are going to live!" Relax. Breathe. Have fun. Enjoy the journey!

God is working his plan and his purposes through us. Marriage is not always what we expect, but it is good. Marriage with kids is messy, but God has a mission. Loving our spouse with kids in the house really is possible. It is loud, busy, and far from what we expected, but it is good because God is at work.

You are going to live! Faithfulness is putting one foot in front of the other. So keep pressing on. And through it all, keep Jesus at the center. No matter where you are, don't give up on the vow to love your spouse with kids in the house.

ACKNOWLEDGMENTS

For Better or for Kids started as an idea on a flight from Detroit to Denver. We would never have imagined at the time that it would grow into a book! In 1998, we started the adventure of marriage as two and have since added four kids, a couple dogs, and a hamster. We are incredibly thankful to God for giving us the opportunity to share our story with so many other couples. We know that, like us, you want to keep your vow to love your spouse with kids in the house!

First, to our own kids in the house—Tyler, Bella, Noah, and Sophia: You have blessed us and enriched our lives in countless ways. We are grateful and proud to be your parents. Thank you for being our biggest fans and cheering your mom and dad on as we have written this book about ALL of us. We love you!

To Patrick's parents: Thank you for modeling Jesus' sacrificial and costly love for almost fifty years of marriage. How sweet it must have been to hear, "Well done, good and faithful servants."

To Ruth's parents: Thank you for believing I could change the world from the moment I was born. Your support, love, and unending encouragement have inspired me to work hard and dream huge. I love you!

Thank you to the readers of The Better Mom and For the Family blogs. We are blessed to be on this journey with each of you and are very thankful for your support. Jesus has given us all the resources we need to love one another faithfully, fully, and forever. Let's keep pressing on together!

Thank you to Esther Fedorkevich, our agent, for your creativity, persistence, and confidence in this book. Without you, this idea would have just stayed an idea. May God give us many more!

Thank you to Amanda Sorenson for your fresh ideas, hard work, coaching, and encouragement. Your time and direction made this project a far better book than we first envisioned. Thank you for your huge contribution to this book!

Finally, to our amazing and talented team at Zondervan: Thank you to Sandy Vander Zicht, Londa Alderink, and Lori Vanden Bosch. We are so thankful for your guidance and encouragement. We are humbled and honored to work with such a great team!

Hoodwinked

Ten Myths Moms Believe & Why We All Need to Knock It Off

Karen Ehman and Ruth Schwenk

PSST ... want to know the secret for being a great mom?

Think she keeps house like June Cleaver, cooks like a Food Network star, and actually *does* all of the things she pins to her Pinterest boards? Oh ... and all while calmly raising her kids *without* ever raising her voice? *Yeah ... right.*

Karen Ehman and Ruth Schwenk have had enough of these misconceptions. Myths such as: "The way I mother is the right (and only) way," "Motherhood is natural, easy, and instinctive," or "My child's bad choice means I'm a bad mom." These myths leave moms hoodwinked and sometimes even heartbroken.

In their straightforward yet encouraging "we've been there" style, Karen and Ruth enable mothers to:

- identify the ten myths of motherhood
- replace the lies with the truth of what God says
- forge healthy, supportive relationships with other moms of all ages and stages
- confidently embrace the calling of motherhood as they care for their families in their own unique way

Ultimately, *Hoodwinked* equips mothers to stop searching for the secret and develop and embrace their relationships instead— with their kids, other mothers, and, most importantly, with God.

A six-session video Bible study for group or individual use is also available.

Available in stores and online!